Landscaping
for Florida's Wildlife
Re-creating Native Ecosystems in Your Yard

Joe Schaefer and **George Tanner**

IFAS Extension Service

University Press of Florida
Gainesville
Tallahassee
Tampa
Boca Raton
Pensacola
Orlando
Miami
Jacksonville

Published in cooperation with the University
Press of Florida

Printed in the United States of America on acid-
free paper

03 02 01   00 99 98   6 5 4 3 2 1

Library of Congress Cataloging-in-Publication Data
Schaefer, Joseph M.
Landscaping for Florida's wildlife: re-creating na-
tive ecosystems in your yard / Joe Schaefer and
George Tanner.
p. cm.
Includes bibliographical references.
ISBN 0-8130-1571-5 (pbk.)
1. Gardening to attract wildlife—Florida. I. Tan-
ner, George Walden. II. Title.
QL59.S35 1997 96-29672
577.5'54'09759—dc21

The University Press of Florida is the scholarly
publishing agency for the State University
System of Florida, comprising Florida A&M
University, Florida Atlantic University, Florida
International University, Florida State
Universtiy, University of Central Florida, Univer-
sity of Florida, University of North Florida,
University of South Florida, and University of
West Florida.

University Press of Florida
15 Northwest 15th Street
Gainesville, FL 32611
http://nersp.nerdc.ufl.edu/~upf

Contents

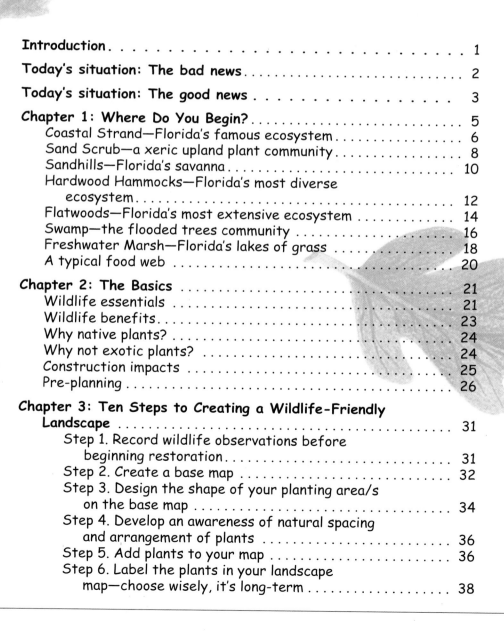

Introduction

Before we get started, we'd like to get you used to some words ecologists use every day, and the ways in which we use them.

Some terms we'll use:

An **ecosystem** is a place where living and nonliving elements interact. In unspoiled conditions, ecosystems gradually blend into each other. They can be distinguished from one another by their soil type and their native plant community.

Living elements include the plants that fix energy from the sun and manufacture food for the other living elements, animals.

Nonliving elements include soil, water, and minerals—all important for the survival of plants and animals.

Ecosystem conservation is an approach humans use to protect, maintain, and restore natural living and nonliving ecosystem elements and their functions at a particular site.

Habitat is that place where a bird or other animal gets the food, cover, water, and space it needs to survive and thrive.

Florida endemics are species found only in Florida.

Exotics are non-native species of plants or animals.

Today's situation:
The bad news

Unfortunately, Florida has more species in danger of extinction than any other state except California and Hawaii. Part of this may be because in Florida, as elsewhere, many efforts to protect wildlife have focused on one species at a time. Management strategies focused only on wildlife that was recreationally or economically important (deer, quail and other game) or those species that were endangered.

This single-species approach has not had a huge success record—and there are several reasons for this lack of effectiveness:

❑ The single-species approach favors a handful of species, often ignoring other species that are members of the same ecosystem.

❑ Single-species strategies focus on wilderness areas, often ignoring developed land (residential and commercial property) where native ecosystems already have been drastically changed by human activity.

Finally, using the single-species approach as a model, property owners have used narrow practices to provide or enhance habitat for wildlife:

❑ Some property owners may plant flowers as nectar sources for *adult butterflies*, but neglect to address the food requirements of *caterpillars* (young butterflies).

❑ Other property owners provide seeds in a bird feeder for cardinals, but use *insecticides* to kill caterpillars and other soft-bodied insects that the cardinals must have to feed their nestlings.

❑ Few property owners do anything for the two dozen bird species and the many other small mammals, reptiles and amphibians that need *tree cavities* or bird houses for nesting, roosting, escaping predators, or avoiding adverse weather conditions.

❑ Fewer still provide *underground burrows* that four dozen species need to satisfy similar life-sustaining requirements.

Lesson learned: A healthy, naturally functioning ecosystem has both food and water for adult and immature creatures—plus places where all creatures can nest or roost, or hide from the elements, and predators.

Today's situation:
The good news

Taking all this into account, there are many opportunities for us to be good stewards of the natural world around us, and serve as contributing members of the ecosystem/s in which we live.

Here's why:

- ❏ It is simple.
- ❏ It can be done year-round.
- ❏ It is inexpensive—we can substitute ingenuity for money.
- ❏ It is convenient—right in our own backyards we can make a difference.
- ❏ It can be as time-consuming or time-enhancing as we choose.
- ❏ It can raise property values—and enjoyment at the same time.
- ❏ It helps us pay the debt we owe those who came before us—and enhance the world of those who follow us.

Here's how:

- ❏ We can follow a kind of Hippocratic oath, by promising ourselves first to do no direct or intentional harm to nature or nature's critters.
- ❏ We can inform ourselves and others about the observable—and hidden—rules of nature.
- ❏ We can restore or put back some of the depleted natural elements for our wild neighbors.

That's where this book comes in. Thank you for reading it.

CHAPTER 1

Where Do You Begin?

One of the first questions you must answer is: which natural plant community or ecosystem is appropriate for your property?

Seven major ecosystems occur throughout Florida: Coastal Strand, Sand Scrub, Sandhills, Hardwood Hammocks, Flatwoods, Swamp, and Freshwater Marsh.

The Florida ecosystems described here are included for these reasons:

❑ One or more of them is indigenous to your area;
❑ The plants associated with these communities can be obtained from your local plant nurseries; and
❑ These plant communities have been successfully restored around the state.

Coastal Strand –
Florida's famous ecosystem

Plant identification list

1. Sea grape
2. Live oak
3. Saw palmetto
4. Coco-plum

The coastal strand *is* Florida to many people—the strand, or **seashore,** attracts millions of visitors every year, the majority of Florida's residents live along the coast—or within a few miles of it.

The narrow but seemingly endless sand dunes of the coastal strand occur parallel and adjacent to most coastal beaches. Now only a few fragmented remnants have been spared from development. Today, Florida's famous ecosystem is dying because of its popularity.

Plants closest to the beach must be tolerant of salt spray. As you move inland, many salt-tolerant plants disappear and the vegetation becomes very similar to the interior scrub community which was actually coastal strand thousands of years ago.

The natural vegetation close to the shore consists of low-growing grasses, vines, and herbaceous plants with a few trees or large shrubs. These trees and shrubs often are stunted and "pruned" due to the wind, salt and blowing sand. Plants which characterize this community are **beach panic grass, sea oats, blanket flower, beach sunflower, sea purslane, beach morning glory, sea grape, cocoplum, inkberry, saw-palmetto, bay cedar, live oak,** and **cabbage palm.**

A variety of **shorebirds** (including threatened **plovers**), **terns** (including threatened **least** and **roseate** species), **gulls, endangered beach mice,** and **endangered sea turtles** nest in these diminishing habitats. Other wildlife associated with interior sand scrub also are found in this seashore community. These include a variety of **lizards, snakes, gopher tortoise,** threatened **scrub jay,** and **threatened kestrel.**

The coastal strand not only provides important habitat for wildlife, but it also regulates wave action and reduces the impact of storm surge from hurricanes—protecting Florida's more interior areas.

Sand Scrub –
a xeric upland plant community

Plant identification list

1. Bear-grass
2. Scrub palmetto
3. Sand pine
4. Myrtle oak
5. Lopsided indiangrass

$S$and scrub is scattered throughout the state on relatively high elevations that are remnants of sand dunes formed when ocean and gulf waters covered most of Florida—about 20 million years ago. They are also home to the greatest number of endemic species.

Scrub communities are easily identified by a dense, but often patchy, layer of shrubs, with patchy ground cover and bare sand. Sometimes pines are absent, with oaks being the dominant trees. Plants characteristic of this community are **oaks, sand pine, bear-grass, gopher apple, saw-palmetto,** and **wild grape.**

Although Florida has much more rainfall than a typical desert, scrub communities are extremely xeric (dry) due to the inability of sand to trap and hold moisture.

Many scrub plants need fire to keep them healthy and to prevent encroachment of plant species from other nearby communities. In the past, a given scrub would naturally burn about every 20 to 40 years, usually from fires started by lightning strikes during summer thunderstorms.

The loose, well-drained soils of scrub allow rapid downward movement of rainwater into Florida's groundwater supplies held in the Floridan aquifer. Unfortunately, this aquifer recharge characteristic also makes sand scrub community a prime target for other uses. Over two-thirds of the original sand scrub communities in Florida have been converted to school campuses, residential and commercial development, citrus, and forestry. As a result, over 25 species of plants and 20 species of wildlife (including sand skink, scrub jay, bluetailed mole skink, gopher tortoise, gopher frog, and Florida mouse) are in danger of extinction.

If you'd like to visit one of the largest remaining relatively intact scrub communities, we recommend the Ocala National Forest in east-central Florida.

Sandhills —
Florida's savanna

Plant identification list

1. Longleaf pine
2. Turkey oak
3. Paw paw
4. Pygmy fringe tree

One of Florida's most interesting habitats is the longleaf pine-turkey oak upland sometimes called a "sandhill." This **xeric (dry) plant community** is found scattered throughout the northern two-thirds of the state. Like the scrub, the yellowish sands of sandhills are well drained, dry, and low in nutrients.

Longleaf pine and **turkey oak** are the most common trees in Florida's sandhills. Other plants include **wiregrass, butterfly pea,** and **gopher apple.** Some animal species found here are the **fox squirrel, gopher tortoise, pocket gopher,** and **fence lizard.**

The sandhill community, like the sand scrub, is fire-maintained. In other words, many of the plants need fire to keep them healthy and to prevent encroachment of plant species from other nearby communities. In the past, a given sandhill would naturally burn about every three to five years. These fires were usually started by **lightning strikes.** However, even **seedling longleaf pine trees** survive frequent, light ground fires.

Without fire, longleaf pine seeds cannot germinate and turkey oaks may become more numerous and larger in size, shading out young pines, shrubs and other species.

Like the sand scrub ecosystem, the loose, well-drained soils of sandhills allow rapid aquifer recharge, making them a prime target for other uses. More than half of the original sandhill communities in Florida have been converted to school campuses, residential and commercial development, citrus, and forestry.

For that reason, the ***southeastern American kestrel, red-cockaded woodpecker, blue-tailed mole skink, eastern indigo snake, Florida mouse*** and the ***short-tailed snake*** are all in jeopardy of extinction.

Hardwood Hammocks –
Florida's most diverse ecosystem

Plant identification list

1. Flowering dogwood
2. American beautyberry
3. Sparkleberry
4. Royal fern
5. Live oak

Hardwood hammocks occur commonly in north-central Florida and sparingly in north and west Florida on rolling terrain. The soils range from poorly to well drained and are high in nutrients containing more organic material and litter than drier sites. The largest historic hammock areas are found near Brooksville, Ocala, and Gainesville.

Hardwood hammock plant communities can be readily identified by thick stands of shade-tolerant hardwoods with few pine trees. In fact, understory vegetation may be quite sparse in older hammocks, as the hardwoods shade out smaller plants.

Some of the most common plants in this community are **black cherry, flowering dogwood, laurel oak, live oak, pignut hickory, American beautyberry, sparkleberry, wild grape,** and **Virginia creeper.** Animal species found here include **southern flying squirrel, gray squirrel, gray fox, white-tailed deer, cardinal, summer tanager, turkey,** and **Carolina wren.**

Close to developed areas, humans have caused many natural sandhills and flatwoods to convert into hammock communities by the self-preserving act of putting out naturally occurring fires. Plants native to sandhills, sand scrub, and flatwoods survive periodic fires quite well. If those fires are suppressed, hammock plants continue to grow and eventually shade out and replace the sandhill and flatwoods community.

Hardwood hammocks occurring on some of the drier soils are often selected for a variety of human uses—these uses include residential and commercial developments, schools, highways, cattle grazing, and forestry. Some wildlife such as the **eastern indigo** and **Florida brown snakes** are in jeopardy of extinction due to alterations of hammocks.

Flatwoods –
Florida's most extensive ecosystem

Plant identification list

1. Saw palmetto
2. Slash pine

Flatwoods occur extensively in the northeastern region of the state, along the Big Bend area (Walton to Levy counties) and to the east and west of the sandy, drier ridges that run north and south through the center of the state to just above the Everglades region in southern Florida. Individual communities may comprise several thousand acres with other, smaller communities—especially wetlands such as *cypress domes* and strands—interspersed throughout.

Flatwoods occur on nearly level land. Water movement to the natural drainages, swamps, ponds, and marshes associated with this community is very gradual. Wet conditions prevail during the rainy season with the water table on or near the surface.

Numerous soil conditions occur in this community:

- ❑ deep
- ❑ acidic
- ❑ poorly drained
- ❑ coarse textured

This community can be readily identified by the flat topography and its slash pine and saw-palmetto vegetation. Typically, the canopy in north Florida flatwoods is more closed than that of the south Florida flatwoods.

Some of the most common plants in this community are *slash pine, live oak, saw-palmetto, wax myrtle, blackberry,* and *gallberry.* Wildlife found here include *gray squirrel, gray fox, white-tailed deer, Bachman's sparrow, eastern meadowlark, pigmy rattlesnake* and *cricket frog.*

Like the hammocks, flatwoods that occur on some of the better-drained, drier soils are often selected for a variety of uses including residential and commercial development, schools, highways, cattle grazing, and forestry. The *indigo snake, southeastern American kestrel,* and *sandhill crane* are all in danger of extinction due to the alteration of flatwoods.

Swamp –
the flooded trees community

Plant identification list

1. Cypress
2. Hackgum
3. Wax myrtle
4. Sweetspire

Swamps occur throughout Florida along rivers and lake margins and mixed in with other communities such as flatwoods. Swamps are located in relatively low areas that are either flooded or saturated part of the year. Their dark soils are poorly drained, and water is at or above ground level a good portion of the year.

Swamps are natural storage areas for floodwater. The plants in these areas also absorb inorganic and organic chemicals from the water, which reduces pollution levels.

Plants in swamp forests often bear fruit at different times than upland plants so wildlife need access to both habitats to have sufficient food year-round. Also, many wildlife species that spend most of their time in uplands depend on these swamps for reproduction. (Treefrogs lay eggs in water but spend their adult life in upland forests. Their ideal landscape has many swamps scattered and available throughout large upland areas.)

Some swamps are dominated by deciduous hardwood trees such as **black gum, red maple,** and **sweet bay.** Other swamps consist mostly of **bald cypress trees**. Other plants characteristic of the swamp include **buttonbush, dahoon holly, cinnamon fern**, and **wax myrtle.**

Animals found in this community are adapted to wet conditions and must be able to survive the flooding that occurs periodically. The trees along the water's edge are also important perch sites for **bald eagles** so they can look over the water for food. Endangered **wood storks** nest in swamps. This is an important ecosystem for the threatened **Florida black bear.**

The extinct **ivory-billed woodpecker** lived in old-aged swamps in Florida but is no longer found in our swamps because all the large old trees were harvested.

Freshwater Marsh –
Florida's lakes of grass

Plant identification list

1. Pickerelweed
2. Maidencare
3. Bulrush

Freshwater marshes are wetlands dominated by rooted herbaceous plants growing in and emerging above shallow water. They make up about one-third of Florida's wetlands and occur most commonly in low, flat, poorly drained areas where the water table is close to the ground surface.

The largest freshwater marsh in Florida is the **Everglades.** Several other large marshes occur along floodplains of the **Kissimmee** and **St. Johns rivers.** Smaller marshes are found throughout the peninsula, especially in small depressions that occur in extensive flatwoods communities.

During the relatively dry winter, especially in south Florida, evaporated water is not replaced by rain and water levels recede. Summer rains usually fill the depressions where marshes occur, but during drought years, some marshes may remain completely dry until torrential rains fill them again.

Ephemeral wetlands are essential habitat for several kinds of frogs and toads because predatory fish cannot live in these sometimes-dry areas.

Fire has always played an important role in the ecology of Florida's marshes. Without fire, marshes become filled by the successional process and are replaced by forests.

Plants characteristic of this ecosystem are **water lilies, pickerelweed, arrowhead, spikerush, maidencane, bulrush, sawgrass,** and **cordgrass.**

Most amphibians and several reptiles depend on marshes. **Alligators** play an important role in creating and maintaining gator holes which provide a water supply for other animals during relatively dry seasons. More than 50 percent of Florida's original marshes have been lost because of draining and filling practices. Today, various animals such as the **snail kite, white ibis, wood stork, sandhill crane** and others associated with marsh ecosystems are in danger of extinction.

A typical food web
Many interactions occur among plants and animals in a healthy ecosystem.

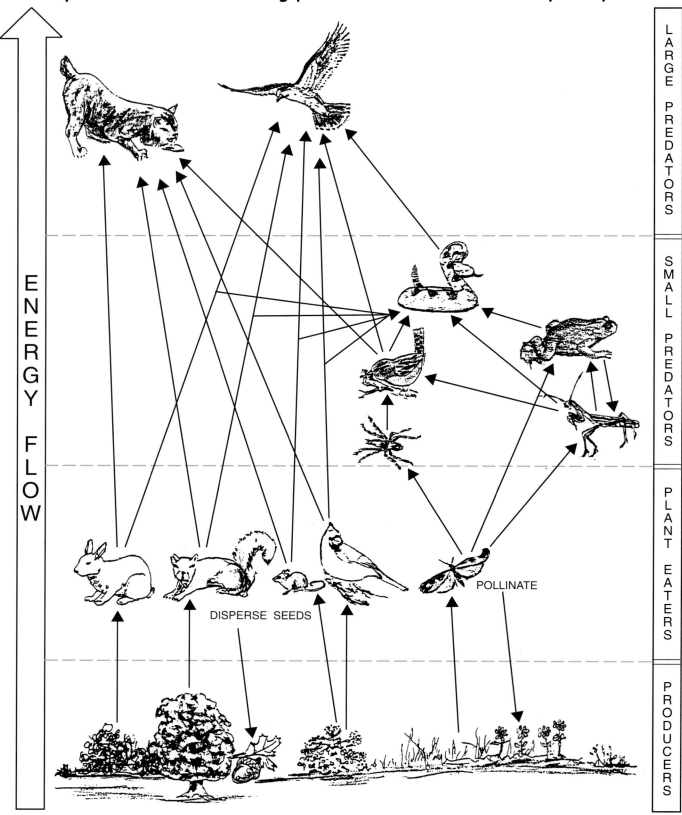

ENERGY FLOW

LARGE PREDATORS

SMALL PREDATORS

PLANT EATERS

PRODUCERS

DISPERSE SEEDS

POLLINATE

CHAPTER 2

The Basics

Wildlife essentials

Food

Plants are the primary source of energy, supporting large, complex **food webs** in any environment. **Plant parts** such as leaves, twigs, bark, roots, fruits, nuts, and seeds are eaten by insects, mammals, and birds which in turn are eaten to sustain larger animals. Some plant parts are available only seasonally and the time of year differs by species. Diets of many wildlife species also change seasonally.

As we mentioned, **cardinals** eat seeds during the fall and winter but switch to soft insects during spring and summer. A site that maintains tall trees, understory trees, tall shrubs, small shrubs, and ground cover will provide better food requirements than an area with only tall trees, because the greatest diversity of native plant species, shape, and size supports the greatest diversity of native wildlife.

Cover

Wildlife species need protection from both predators and weather. Cover also helps restrict the amount of food available at any time to each level in a given food web so that the energy flow will be sustained generation after generation. Example: *if all bird nests were highly visible to predators, every egg and nestling would be eaten and no offspring would be available to continue the important balance between predators and prey.*

Cover requirements are almost as diverse as food requirements and can be provided by both plant and **non-plant habitat elements.**

❑ Some insects feed on the underside of leaves to reduce detection;

❑ dozens of birds, mammals, reptiles and amphibians use **tree cavities** for nesting (woodpeckers) and sleeping (treefrogs);

❑ about four dozen species use underground burrows for nesting, sleeping, and hiding.

An ecosystem approach to landscaping would include preserving the greatest diversity of plants, **underground burrows**, and **dead trees** (or 10-foot-tall stumps of dead trees [**snags**] which will not present liability hazards). If dead trees are removed, some of the cover requirements they provided can be replaced by installing **bird houses.**

Water

Fresh water is essential for most wildlife. Many species need to drink water and other species such as frogs and toads require standing water during all or some parts of the year to complete part of their **life cycles.** A water source on one piece of property may be critical to all wildlife living in the entire neighborhood.

While traditional, elevated ground-level bird baths are accessible only to birds. A pond with gently sloping sides allows many kinds of wildlife to choose different depths to satisfy their requirements. Even small depressions in rocks or soil that retain water only temporarily help to satisfy wildlife water requirements.

Space: territory, home range, and vertical space

An animal's need for space is simply the size of area containing sufficient food, cover, and water for the creature to survive. This size varies depending on the density and availability of these resources.

Common terms for expressing **space needs** are

"territory," the area defended by an animal and

"home range," the area the animal actually uses for life-sustaining needs.

> Examples of space needs are:
>
> 100 miles^2 for a Florida panther,
>
> 2 miles^2 for a white-tailed deer in north Florida, and
>
> 1 acre for a cardinal.

Most Florida wildlife species are not able to satisfy their spatial requirements on a typical residential lot. If neighbors (or the builder/contractor or developer) agree to arrange remaining natural areas on each property in a neighborhood so that they are adjacent to one another, larger intact better quality habitats can be salvaged.

This adjacency approach reduces the overall impact of construction and development much more effectively than retaining or creating several small, isolated areas, one to a lot. The same philosophy can be used to maintain critical habitat features for larger animals, ones that are often fragmented when parcels of rural acreage are subdivided.

Many species also have vertical space requirements. Some, such as the **American crow**, nest high in tall trees but feed on the ground. Others, like the **hooded warbler** and **brown thrasher**, nest close to the ground but feed in understory trees.

Wildlife benefits

While the cumulative effects of many property owners individually landscaping for wildlife can be enormous, look what its rewards are for you:

Landscaping for wildlife can provide the priceless daily experience of watching birds and other wild animals. But that's not all! Landscaping for wildlife can also reduce property maintenance time and costs, contribute to a cleaner environment, help to reduce exotic plant infestations, and restore homes for many animals that once lived on your property.

What will actually be involved—besides the ecosystem research described earlier?

Keep focused on the best practices. Wildlife professionals focus on maintaining and/or restoring as much of the native ecosystem as possible. This is the approach they use in public natural areas throughout Florida; this is the approach you can easily adapt to your property.

Visualize what landscaping for wildlife could mean to you if you replace an existing lawn with native plantings that reduce both the time and money spent on lawn maintenance: It is a fact that the average Florida homeowner spends from $100 (do-it-yourself-maintenance) to over $1,000 (professional maintenance) just for feeding, weeding and grooming the lawn on an average-size residential lot. And the bigger the property, the larger the budget item for upkeep.

Why native plants?

Native plants often have fewer pest and disease problems than lawns and exotic ornamental plants. Because natives are also adapted to local temperature and rainfall patterns, they require less watering and fertilizing to maintain sound health. Native plants provide better nutritional requirements and are the basis for delicately balanced food webs.

Selecting native plants for landscaping also is ecologically responsible. In Florida, about **900 exotic plants** have been added to the choices of plants used to beautify developed areas. Of these, about 400 plants have already invaded natural areas where they aggressively compete with Florida natives.

Why not exotic plants?

Unfortunately, many exotics flourish in Florida—driving native plants away. Several of the most aggressive plants have drastically changed the landscape both ecologically and visually.

Examples: *In North Florida, the most aggressive non-native is the* ***kudzu vine****, Pueraria lobata. Kudzu vine can turn a small pine forest into a green nightmare in just a few years. It looks inviting to us humans, but there is nothing left for the native wildlife. The kudzu vine has created a "desert" for them.*

Another destroyer of habitat and wildlife is ***melaleuca****, Melaleuca quinquenervia. Melaleuca was purposely introduced into South Florida as a landscape tree, earlier in this century, to stop soil erosion. Little did they know.*

Melaleuca—the birch-like tree that's always dropping its bark, spreads like wildfire—in fact, wildfire spreads it! Huge areas of south Florida—and now central Florida—are becoming melaleuca monocultures (land dominated by one plant species). There is a war on melaleuca being waged on **Sanibel Island***, where it, together with another purposely introduced exotic, the so-called* **Brazilian pepper** *(Schinus terebinthifolius) tree have taken over acre after acre of native coastal strand —threatening the life-supporting systems of Sanibel's fabled wildlife.*

We are learning the hard way that as plant communities change, animal populations also change. We know now that very few species use melaleuca monocultures, very few use Brazilian pepper monocultures. We are currently spending millions of dollars each year trying to control the spread of these exotic or non-native species in Florida. We are literally locking the garden gate after the animals have fled.

Ben Franklin once said, "An ounce of prevention is worth a pound of cure." By using native species, we know we are not contributing to the future frustration and expense of waging war on introduced exotics.

Construction impacts

Many popular construction and development practices remove the food, cover, water, and space requirements for birds and other wildlife. The cumulative impact is that populations of native wildlife species are experiencing severe reductions and even extinctions at site, neighbor-hood, county, regional, and state levels.

What we are learning is that we do not always have to destroy wildlife habitats completely to satisfy our own human food, cover, water, and space needs.

One of the best things responsible property owners can do to pre-serve their natural heritage is to replace unessential developed areas with good wildlife habitat. This will help developed properties to blend with natural areas. This will replace the stark contrast between wild-life-suitable and wildlife-unsuitable areas currently existing in many regions in Florida.

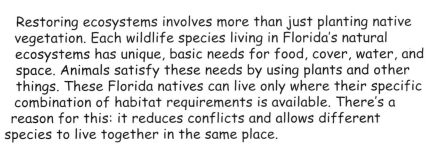

Restoring ecosystems involves more than just planting native vegetation. Each wildlife species living in Florida's natural ecosystems has unique, basic needs for food, cover, water, and space. Animals satisfy these needs by using plants and other things. These Florida natives can live only where their specific combination of habitat requirements is available. There's a reason for this: it reduces conflicts and allows different species to live together in the same place.

Most large natural areas provide diverse habitat characteristics that can satisfy the needs of dozens of individuals of more than 100 different wildlife species. The maximum number of native wildlife species maintained or returned on an individual residential or commercial site can be achieved by providing the greatest possible diversity of food, cover, water, and space requirements.

Where environmentally sound land management has been used, win-win situations develop. More and more, low-maintenance, wildlife-friendly restorations find favor with buyers and sellers. Next question: how does this all work?

Pre-planning

We are soon going to take you where you want to end up, but let's go over the planning process—as Mary Beth Lacey observed, "Prior planning prevents poor performance."

First, identify your property's native plant community from those listed earlier in Chapter 1. If you are looking for greater detail than provided here, more resources are listed in Chapter 5.

How do you find out which ecosystem best matches your location?

❑ You can check some of the sketches and descriptions here.
❑ You can do research.
❑ You can check with the experts.

First, look at the sketches and descriptions that follow.

Identification of ecosystem(s) is based on:

- ❑ the general ecosystem distribution maps found in the references in Chapter 5.
- ❑ county soil survey located at the local U.S. Dept. of Agriculture Natural Resources Conservation Service office or your local library. (*This document provides maps of the soil types in your county and a discussion of the ecosystems naturally occurring on these respective soil types.*)
- ❑ the original ecosystem present before development of your property; **local county foresters** also might have records of original ecosystem boundaries in your area and can make recommendations on ecosystem selection for your property.
- ❑ the type of soil on the property. (*Note: In many cases the original soil has been significantly altered and may no longer be suitable for the type of plants that originally occurred on the site. Your local Extension Service office will provide you with information about testing your soil to determine if it is suitable for different plants.*)
- ❑ the most common natural ecosystem/s found in local natural areas (visit your state and county parks).
- ❑ existing native vegetation that may be characteristic of one of the natural systems.
- ❑ Observations over time. **Example**: *If standing surface water persists for several hours after a rainfall, and the soil turns muddy on any specific sites, these areas are good candidates for wetland ecosystems.*

Example: Slash pine growing in either a grassland or forest condition might indicate a Flatwoods community. This community usually occurs on level land, is poorly drained, and contains saw-palmetto as an understory plant.

> Once you have identified your soil type and native ecosystem you are ready to move to the next phase: figuring out what's missing, what your choices are, and how much or how little restoration you want to aim for.

In the second phase. Evaluate your on- and off-property considerations.

Manageable size: The area you select to landscape will require weeding and watering during the first year. Temperature, the amount of rainfall, use of weed-barriers and irrigation systems will influence how much time you will have to spend maintaining your planted area. Make sure you don't overcommit yourself with so much work that you spoil your enjoyment of this activity.

Aesthetics: Plants associated with native ecosystems may not provide the same aesthetic appeal as exotic ornamentals in your neighborhood—especially if your neighborhood is one that has been redesigned. If you want your property to blend in with the neighborhood, make some compromises. (**Example:** *Landscape the front, most visible parts of your property like the neighborhood standard with some native plants mixed in. Devote your major attention to restoring the ecosystem in less visible areas.*)

Utilities: Ask your utilities companies to locate underground utilities to avoid digging into telephone lines, electric and television cables, irrigation, and water pipes. Before you plant tall-growing trees, check the locations of overhead utility lines.

Drainage patterns: Before making your final landscaping plans, wait until after a good rain. If the ground in any area retains standing water or if it is spongy an hour after the rain has stopped, plants that naturally grow on drier sites should be planted elsewhere.

Connections between uplands (dry) and wet areas: Many wildlife species need access to both water and upland habitats for food and cover. (*Example: Treefrogs lay eggs in water and their immature tadpoles live in water for weeks before emerging as adults and spending the rest of their lives in trees. Freshwater turtles live in the water most of the time, but one day of the year, the female must travel into sandy upland areas to dig a hole and lay her eggs.*) Maintaining native conditions in uplands adjacent to wetlands will help to assure access to habitats required for the entire life cycles of these species. You can help provide for this by planting emergent and shoreline vegetation in and adjacent to aquatic areas to provide food and cover for many wildlife species. Travel corridors from uplands to existing water supplies such as ponds and streams on or adjacent to the site will allow access by many species.

Existing vegetation: Before some of the understory, shade-tolerant plants can be installed, let existing trees provide necessary shade. Be mindful that the extensive root systems of well-established trees may compete with new plants, causing you to water more frequently. And some roots of some existing plants may have to be cut simply to make room for the new ones. However, try to avoid damaging more than a third of the root system. Use common sense, too. When using the plant tables (chapter 4) note that plants requiring sunny (S) locations will not do well if planted in the shade of tall trees.

Adjacent land use: If any property that is protected from future development is adjacent to your property, try locating your ecosystem restoration near it. This increases the size of the area providing diverse habitat requirements, enabling it to accommodate more species.

Wildlife requirements available in the neighborhood: Inventory existing habitat requirements in your neighborhood.

- ❑ What types of foods are already available?
- ❑ Is there a good diversity of native plants producing fruits, nuts, and seeds?
- ❑ Is there a water source just for birds or one that addresses many wildlife species' needs?
- ❑ How about dead trees or bird houses?
- ❑ What is the cover and space situation like?
- ❑ Are several layers of native vegetation available?

Your landscaping efforts can be most effective if you concentrate on providing those requirements lacking in your neighborhood. For example, maybe there is enough food, water, and space in your neighborhood for a great-crested flycatcher and all they need is cover (a bird house) for the area to be suitable for them.

> Before you embark on Steps 1-10 remember you don't have to restore everything all at once. Your efforts will take time to show up. Your success, over time, will be measured by how you adapt your vision to the reality of your natural ecosystem and to the increases in wildlife abundance and variety.

CHAPTER 3

Ten Steps to Creating a Wildlife-Friendly Landscape

Step 1. Record wildlife observations before beginning restoration

If you are landscaping to try to help wildlife, how will you know if you have succeeded?

The best way —before you implement your plan—is to determine how many animals and which species are using your property and then to monitor wildlife use yearly after you begin landscaping for wildlife. Use field guides listed in chapter 6 to help you identify animals.

As a guide to the present—and the possible—we have included a chapter (**Chapter 7**) on the major groups of animals found in Florida: some of the 500 bird, 94 mammal, 88 reptile, and 51 amphibian species.

As the plant community in your restored ecosystem grows and matures, you will be able to detect changes in abundance and diversity of animals. The occurrence of more animals would mean that through your landscaping efforts more food, cover, water, and space needs have become available.

You can prepare your own system of recording this information or use the Wildlife Observations Recording Form provided in **Chapter 5**.

Step 2. Create a base map

Use the template in **Chapter 5** (page 74), to create a base map for your entire property—or at least the area you want to restore to a native habitat. You may need to adjust the scale of the map to fit your property's relative size or develop several smaller maps of greater detail—but it's a good place to start.

What other resources can you use?

❑ A *long measuring tape* (at least 100 feet) is handy.

❑ Your *property survey map* shows accurate locations of your house as well as property lines.

❑ *Utility companies* can mark electric, telephone, TV cable, sewer, and water pipes and lines. *Note: If you have irrigation pipes, septic tanks, underground fuel tanks, or drain fields, place them on your map. You'll find this useful for other purposes as well.*

Tips and Techniques

To increase the ease and accuracy of transferring visual information to your map, lay out a checkerboard grid on the ground using stakes and string.

Connect your grid to a permanent object with a baseline so you can reconstruct your grid at a later date **(Figure 1)**.

Once you have created your grid and established a reference point (such as the corner of your house) that will be easy to find again, all other objects can be easily and accurately located using an X,Y coordinate system.

*Example: using a scale of 6 feet on the ground=1/2 inch on the map, the tree in **Figure 1** would be 18 feet to the west and 6 feet to the north of the northwest corner of the house. Note: Your base map should reflect all existing trees, overhead and underground utilities, buildings, patios, pools, sidewalks, drive-ways, and other use areas such as clotheslines and play areas .*

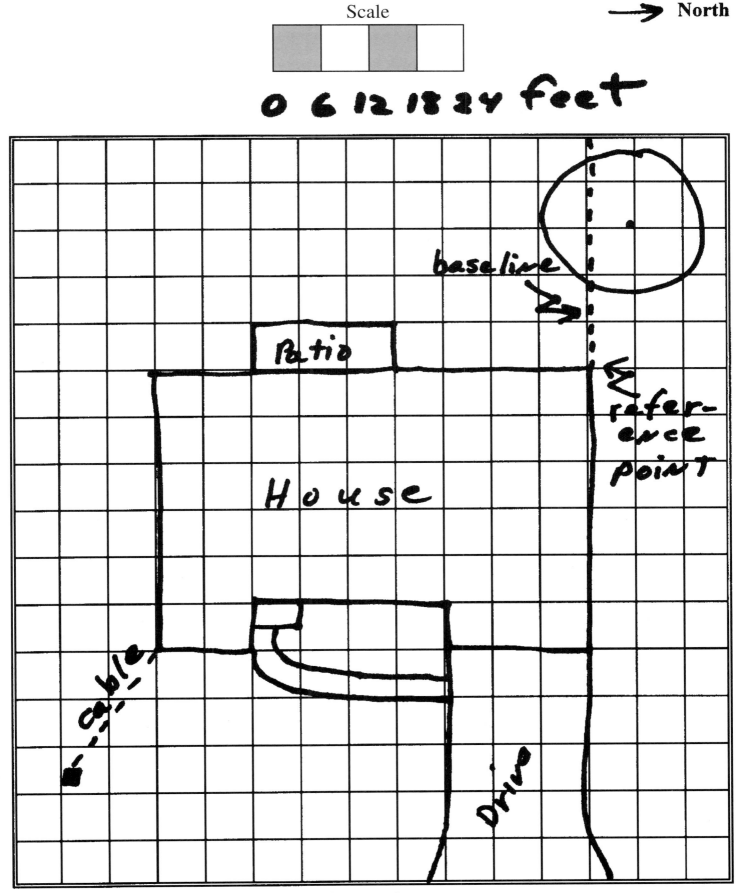

Scale

0 6 12 18 24 feet

North

baseline

reference point

Patio

House

cable

Drive

Figure 1. Base map with baseline, reference points and existing objects.

Step 3. Design the shape of your planting area/s on the base map

First, see what the most common human-made landscape style is in your neighborhood. Is it a pattern of plants around the house foundation and borders along sidewalks and driveways? At the other extreme is it a natural style with no lawn? You'll have to decide whether you want your property to blend in with your neighbors' or whether you want to start a trend, whether you want your front yard and side yards to blend in, and restore just your backyard.

Larger property owners may want to designate a portion of land around a wetland, or adjacent to an existing undisturbed tract, to restore habitat features.

Tips and Techniques

Use these resources:

❑ landscape books in your local library,
❑ landscape architects,
❑ plant nurseries, and
❑ local Extension Service horticulture agents and Master Gardener volunteers.

Once you have decided on a particular style, draw the rough outlines of your planting areas on your map (Figure 2).

0 6 12 18 24 feet

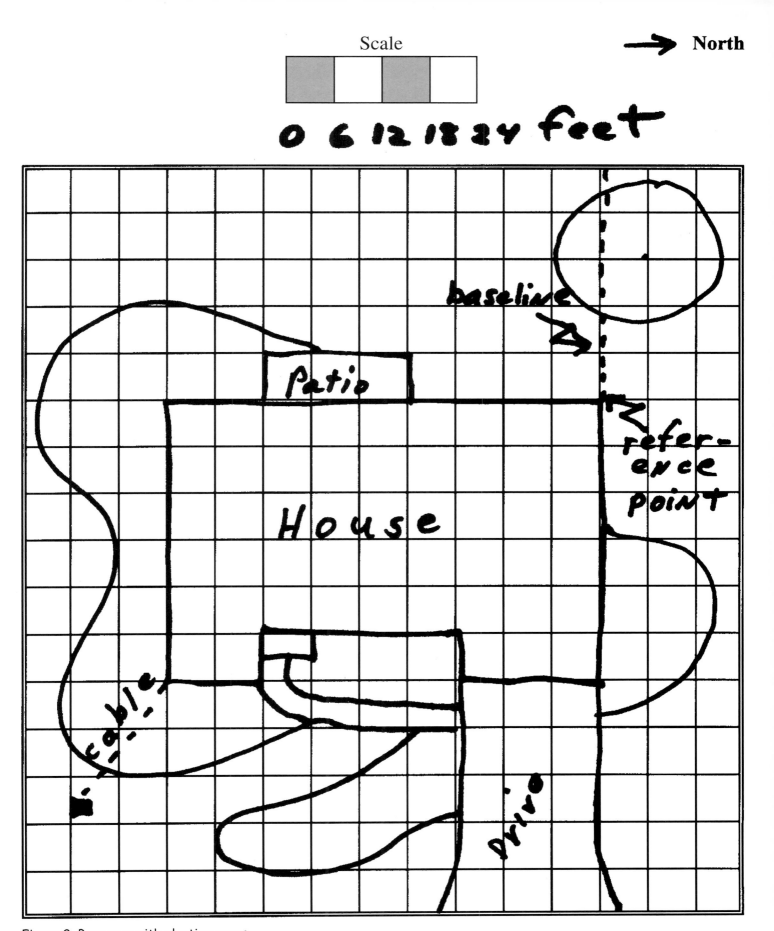

Figure 2. Base map with planting areas.

Step 4. Develop an awareness of natural spacing and arrangement of plants

Example: In a mature hardwood hammock ecosystem, tall trees of various species are spaced about 20 feet apart. They form a dense canopy with their high branches touching each other, while sun-loving understory plants bunch together wherever there is available light.

In contrast, the dominant large trees in a sandhill ecosystem, longleaf pines, are spaced far apart but do not form a dense canopy because their branches are short and their needles are sparsely arranged at the branch tips.

Tips and Techniques

Visit public park preserves where the ecosystem you have identified for your property is maintained in the natural condition. Walk around, take pictures and notes, make sketches. Notice plant arrangements and the elements that might provide wildlife habitat. Florida's Department of Environmental Protection (DEP) has a brochure identifying locations of all state parks. There are 113 in Florida. Information about some of them is available doing a key word search from http://www.dept.state.fl.us/information.htm l). This information is also available on the Internet (http://www.dep.state.fl.usl)

Step 5. Add plants to your map

Now that you know which ecosystem is yours and what the natural plant arrangement is like, you are ready to add suitable plants to your map **(Figure 3).**

At this point, you are not choosing the species of plants, just the structure (tall tree, small tree, tall shrub, small shrub, etc.). **Use circles with the following diameters:**

> **tall trees—24 feet (4 squares on the base map)**
>
> **small trees—15 feet (2$^1/_2$ squares on the base map)**
>
> **tall shrubs—9 feet (1$^1/_2$ squares on the base map)**
>
> **small shrubs—3 feet ($^1/_2$ square on the base map)**

Make sure to layer plants for a variety of vertical heights (for example, shrubs and small trees can be placed under tall trees). Aim to mimic the natural plant arrangement. Remember that understory shrubs should increase in numbers and cover over time.

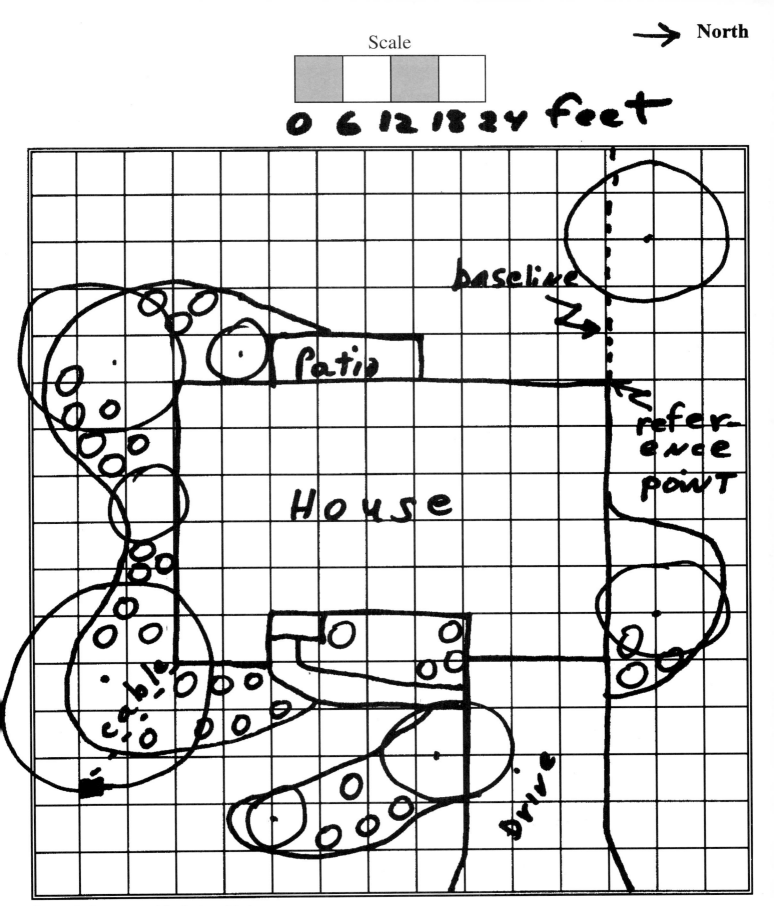

Scale

0 6 12 18 24 feet

North

baseline

reference point

Patio

House

Drive

Figure 3. Base map with plants added.

Step 6. Label the plants in your landscape map—choose wisely, it's long-term

Find the lists of plants in Chapter 4 associated with the ecosystem you have identified for your property. Make sure to choose plants that are characteristic of your ecosystem *(indicated with an * in each plant list)*. Then select a variety of species from each structure category (e.g., small shrub, tall shrub, etc.) **(Figure 4)**.

During your selection process, consider soil types, drainage patterns, shade, fruiting season of the plant, and, especially for trees, their mature height.

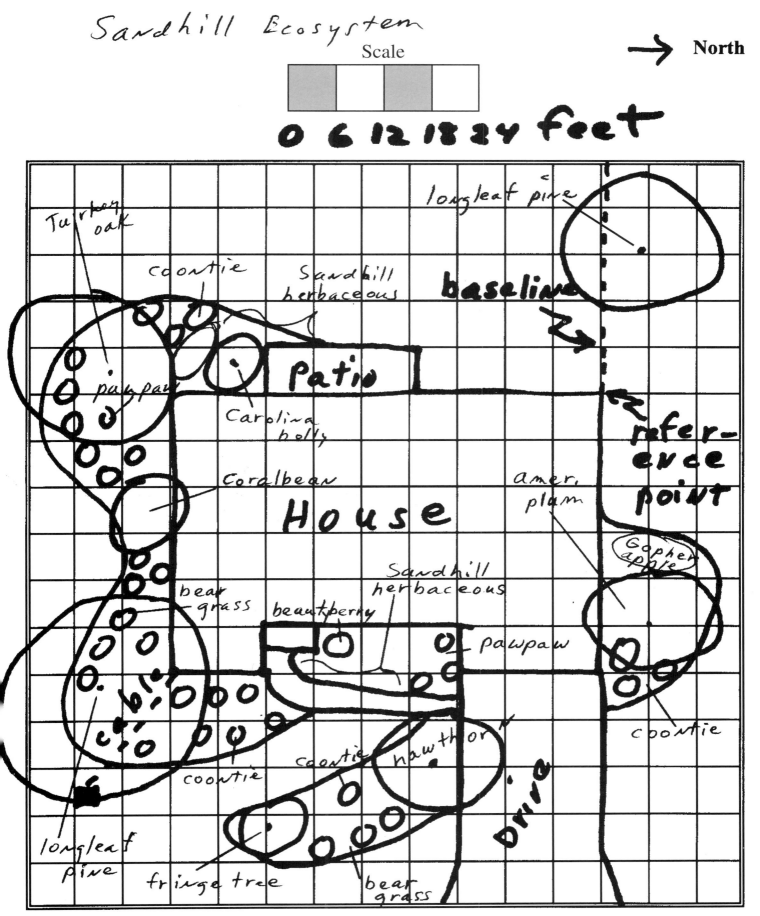

Figure 4. Base map with plants labeled.

Step 7. Add non-plant elements

Here are some non-plant features that will help to restore some of the original habitat values of your property.

Burrows: They provide unique shelter that is relatively cool in summer and warm in winter and are good refuges from predators. Amphibians like them because they are also relatively damp.

How to: Add this habitat element by using a 5-inch-wide lightweight, corrugated, flexible, pre-drilled, black plastic drain pipe, cut to a 10-foot length. This costs a few dollars at a local building supply store.

Look for a site on your property in a relatively dry area—no smaller than 3' by 8'—that doesn't flood during normal rainfalls. Install this "burrow" by digging a trench wide enough for the black ridged pipe and about 3 feet deep at the center and gradually sloping upward to the ground surface (like a wide letter 'V'). Then place the pipe in the trench with drain holes facing down and backfill, covering it with the soil you dug up.

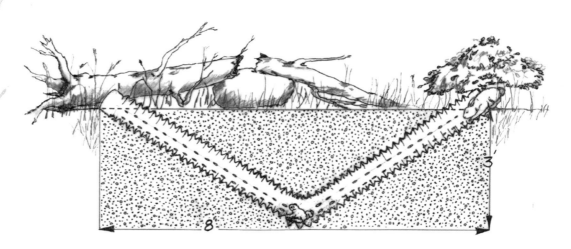

Bird houses: Many species (woodpeckers, Carolina chickadees, etc.) nest only in trees or cavities. Eastern bluebirds and others roost in cavities during winter cold spells. Squirrels, bats, mice, treefrogs and several other types of animals have also been found in bird houses.

See the Florida Cooperative Extension Service Fact Sheet, *Helping Cavity-nesters in Florida* (SS-WIS-901). (Available at your county Extension office and on the Internet, http://www.wec.ufl.edu/extension/.)

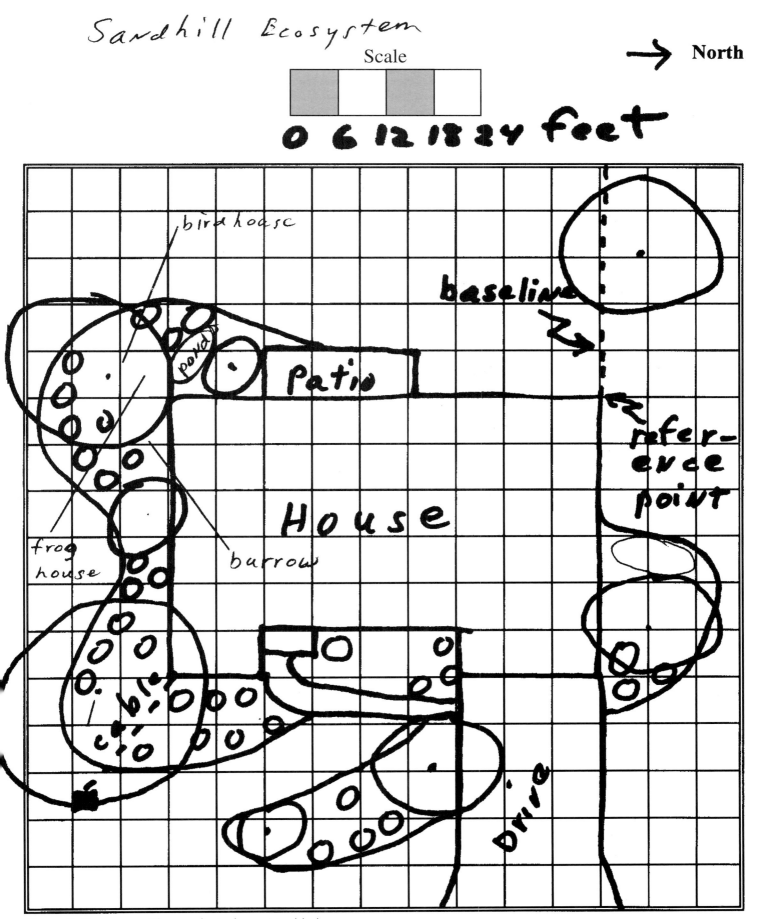

Scale

North

0 6 12 18 24 feet

Sandhill Ecosystem

- bird house
- baseline
- reference point
- pond
- Patio
- House
- frog house
- burrow
- drive

Figure 5. Base map with non-plant elements added.

Treefrog houses: Treefrogs (15 species in Florida alone!) rest in places out of the drying sun . They naturally seek out cracks in trees, but also will adapt to many artificial crevices such as a 3-foot-long, 1.5-inch plastic PVC pipe stuck in the ground (preferably in a shaded place). Treefrogs will climb up the outside of the pipe, crawl into the top and rest, while they hold on to the smooth inside of the pipe with their suction-cup toes. You can paint the pipe to blend into its surroundings.

Rock and brush piles: Reptiles and other small animals need cover. On cool mornings, reptiles increase their temperature lying on sun-warmed rocks. You can beautify your brush pile by planting flowering vines (see Chapter 4) that will climb over the branches. *Caution: be careful which vines you plant. Some, like* **air potato vines**—*an invasive, exotic species —take over.*

Ponds: Because a pond will benefit so many different kinds of animals, it is probably the most important non-plant element you can add to your ecosystem. Large animals drink from ponds. Insects, frogs, and salamanders depend on ponds as sites for egg laying and growth of larvae or young. Butterflies suck water out of wet soil along the edge of the pond. And we all know how birds and other animals like to bathe in the shallow water of ponds. If you create a pond that provides different habitats and water depths, it will benefit the greatest variety of critters.

Tips and Techniques

- ❑ Ponds do not have to be huge—even a 3-foot-diameter pond will add tremendous habitat values.
- ❑ Just like swimming pools, ponds can be freeform or pre-formed.
- ❑ Freeform ponds can be made out of concrete or flexible liners from materials such as synthetic rubber and propylene polymers.

Pre-formed fiberglass or plastic ponds of various shapes are available at local building supply and department stores. A disadvantage of these pre-formed types is that unless they have gently sloping sides birds cannot use them to bathe and some animals, such as turtles, may not be able climb out of these ponds easily.

You can build a pile of rocks to create a shallow area for birds (less than 2 inches deep) and lean a board or log on the side for turtles and frogs to climb out on.

Step 8. Prepare a materials list and estimate costs BEFORE you shop

Before you start buying all of the plants, bird houses, etc., that you have planned to install, it is a good idea first to see how much all of this is going to cost. The Plant and Non-Plant Materials Cost Forms in **Chapter 5**, will help you to organize this information.

Tips and Techniques

❑ Copy the forms in this book so you'll always have master forms.

❑ Use these forms when you visit a plant nursery to familiarize yourself with stock availability, prices, and sizes.

❑ At a nursery, the cost of trees and shrubs is more a function of the volume of the container it's growing in than the plant's height.

❑ Contact several nurseries to determine plant availability and costs or

❑ Refer to the most recent edition of the Plantfinder, published by Betrock, 1601 N. Palm Ave. Suite 303, Pembroke Pines, FL 33026 (954/438-2620; FAX 954/438-2632).

❑ If the estimated cost of your landscape plan is more than your budget, you have several choices:

— Make your plan less ambitious or less detailed.

— Do more of the work yourself.

— Break your plan into pieces and install in phases—beginning with the slowest-growing plants.

— Do one area, phase the others in later.

— If your properties adjoin. consider sharing some of labor and costs with a like-minded neighbor.

Step 9. Install plants and non-plant elements of the ecosystem

Installing the elements of your habitat requires more effort than just placing plants in holes. Look back at your landscape map, where you have indicated specific places for each woody plant. You can locate the exact spot on the ground for each plant by reversing the process you followed in **Step 2** to create a map of plants and other objects that existed on the ground.

Your newly installed habitat ecosystem may look a little sparse at first. But remember, plants take a while to grow and to fill out the empty spaces. If you plant too densely instead of according to the natural plant arrangement design, you may have problems later because of overcrowding. Detailed information about soil suitability, selecting healthy plants at the nursery, watering, diseases, insect pests, mulches, etc. can be found in the following University of Florida publication:

Black B. J. and K. C. Ruppert. 1995. *Your Florida Landscape: A guide to planting and maintenance.* University of Florida Cooperative Extension Service. SP 135. 287 pp.

You may want to consult with a local Master Gardener group to receive guidance on planting and plant maintenance procedures. You can reach your local Master Gardener group through your local IFAS extension office.

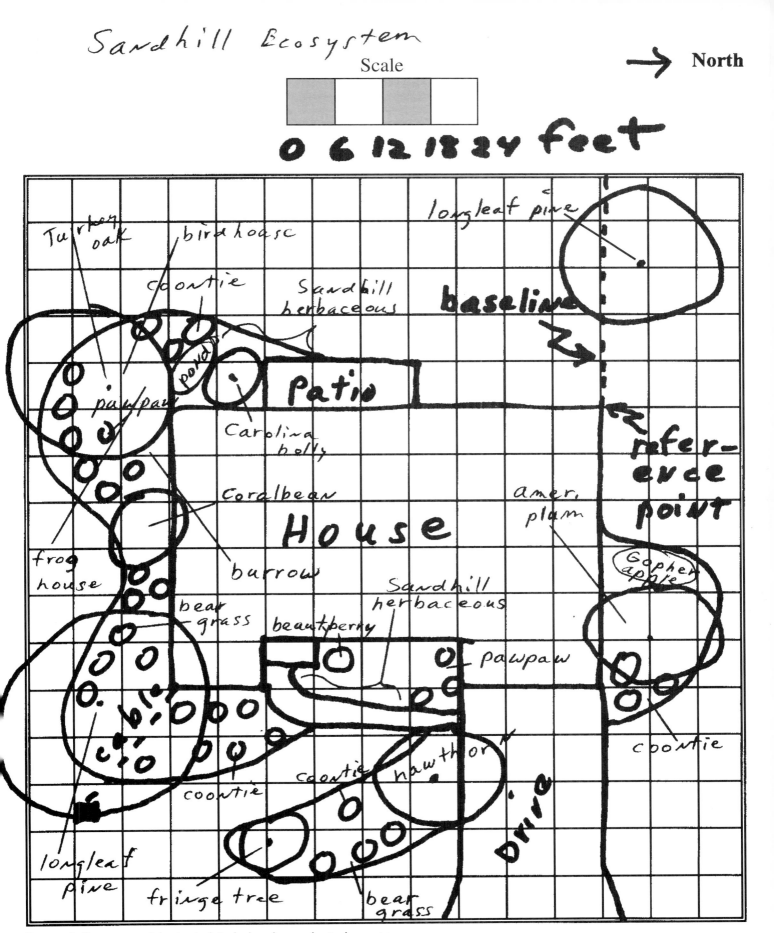

Figure 6. Base map with plants labeled and non-plant elements.

Step 10. Maintain your habitat

Your planting is done—at least the first phase of it. Now, you'll have to take care of your newly installed plants, paying close attention to their water needs. The first month after transplantation is the critical month: your new plants are in shock from the move and replanting, and they are going to have to get used to a new watering regime.

Watering plants individually conserves water—even though it takes more time. If you've planted during the wet season, you'll spend less time watering because a day with more than an inch of rainfall can replace a watering day. Keep this schedule in mind:

Watering Schedule	Weeks 1 & 2	Weeks 3 to 10	Months 4 to 10
	Daily	3 times/wk	Once/wk

Other important maintenance activities the first year will include keeping mulch on the planting beds and removing or weeding exotic plants. If native species other than the ones you plant appear as a result of seeds planted from bird droppings, squirrels, etc., you can chose to leave or remove them according to how they fit into your plan.

Checklist of steps involved in landscaping for wildlife

- ❑ Step 1. Wildlife observations
- ❑ Step 2. Create base map
- ❑ Step 3. Design shape of the planting area
- ❑ Step 4. Become aware of natural look
- ❑ Step 5. Add plants
- ❑ Step 6. Label plants
- ❑ Step 7. Add non-plants
- ❑ Step 8. Prepare materials list
- ❑ Step 9. Install plants
- ❑ Step 10. Maintain

ADDITIONAL READING:

Cerulian, S., C. Botha, and D. Legare. 1987. *Planting a refuge for wildlife.* Florida Game and Fresh Water Fish Commission, Nongame Wildlife Program and USDA Soil Conservation Service. 33 pp.

CHAPTER 4

Plant Lists for Florida's Major Ecosystems

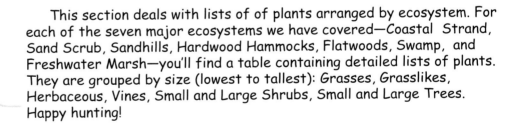

This section deals with lists of of plants arranged by ecosystem. For each of the seven major ecosystems we have covered—Coastal Strand, Sand Scrub, Sandhills, Hardwood Hammocks, Flatwoods, Swamp, and Freshwater Marsh—you'll find a table containing detailed lists of plants. They are grouped by size (lowest to tallest): Grasses, Grasslikes, Herbaceous, Vines, Small and Large Shrubs, Small and Large Trees. Happy hunting!

Coastal Strand Plant Tables

COASTAL STRAND GRASSES

Scientific Name	Common Name	Range	Mature Height	Light Requirement	Wildlife Value Food	Wildlife Value Cover
Andropogon virginicus	Broomsedge bluestem	N,C,S	6 ft	S, PSh	—	—
Distichlis spicata	Seashore saltgrass ST	N,C,S	0.5 ft	S	—	—
Eragrotis spectabilis	Purple lovegrass	N,C,S	2 ft	S, PSh	—	—
Panicum amarum	Beach panic grass ST *	N,C,S	1-2 ft	S	—	—
Uniola paniculata	Sea oats ST *	N,C,S	3-5 ft	S	—	—

COASTAL STRAND HERBACEOUS

Scientific Name	Common Name	Range	Mature Height	Light Requirement	Wildlife Value Food	Wildlife Value Cover
Aster spp.	Aster	N,C,S	1-4 ft	S	—	—
Borrichia arborescens	Silver sea oxeye ST	S	2-4 ft	S	—	—
Commelina spp.	Day flower	N,C,S	2 ft	S, PSh	—	—
Crotonopsis linearis	Rushfloil	N,C,S	0.5-1 ft	S	—	—
Gaillardia pulchella	Blanket flower ST *	N,C,S	1-1.5 ft	S, PSh	—	—
Helianthus debilis	Beach sunflower ST *	N,C,S	1-2 ft	S	—	—
Heterotheca subaxillaris	Camphorweed	N,C,S	2-4 ft	S	—	—
Lippia noriflora	Matchweed ST	N,C,S	0.5 ft	S	—	—
Okenia hypogaea	Beach peanut ST	S	0.5 ft	S	—	—
Portulaca pilosa	Portulaca	N,C,S	3-8 ft	S	—	—
Sesuvium portulacastrum	Sea purslane ST *	N,C,S	1-1.5 ft	S	—	—
Solidago spp.	Goldenrod	N,C,S	2-4 ft	S, PSh	—	—
Tradescantia spp.	Spiderwort	N,C,S	2 ft	S, PSh	—	—
Verbena maritima	Beach verbena ST	S	0.5-1 ft	S	—	—
Veronia spp.	Ironweed	N,C,S	2-4 ft	S, PSh	—	—

COASTAL STRAND VINES

Scientific Name	Common Name	Range	Mature Height	Light Requirement	Wildlife Value Food	Wildlife Value Cover
Ampelopsis arborea	Peppervine I	N,C,S	—	S, PSh	—	—
Centrosoma virginianum	Butterfly pea	N,C,S	—	S, PSh	—	—
Ipomoea pes-caprae	Railroad vine ST *	S	—	S	—	—
Ipomoea stolonifera	Beach morning glory ST *	N,C,S	—	S	—	—
Vitis spp.	Wild grape	N,C,S	—	S, PSh, Sh	—	—

RANGE:
    N = North Florida, C = Central Florida, S = South Florida
LIGHT REQUIREMENTS:
    S = Sun, Sh = Shade, PSh = Partial Shade

* = Plants characteristic of Coastal Strand
ST = Salt tolerant   I = Irritant plant
WILDLIFE VALUES:
    L = Low, M = Medium, H = High

COASTAL STRAND SHRUBS

Scientific Name	Common Name	Range	Mature Height	Light Requirement	Wildlife Value Food	Wildlife Value Cover
Small Shrubs						
Baccharis halimifolia	Salt Bush ST	N,C,S	5-7 ft	S	L	H
Borrichia arborescens	Silver sea oxeye ST	S	2-4 ft	S	M	M
Ceratiola ericoides	Rosemary ST	N,C,S	4-5 ft	S	L	L
Chiococca alba	Snowberry ST	C,S	6-9 ft	S	H	H
Chrysobalanus icaco	Coco-plum ST *	S	15 ft	S	H	H
Licania michauxii	Gopher apple	N,C	0.5-1 ft	S, PSh	H	L
Lycium carolinianum	Christmas berry ST	N,C,S	6-8 ft	S, PSh	H	H
Scaevola plumieri	Inkberry ST *	C,S	1-6 ft	S	H	M
Yucca filamentosa	Bear grass	N,C,S	2-4 ft	S	M	M
Zamia spp.	Coontie	N,C,S	3 ft	S, PSh	L	L
Large Shrubs						
Forestiera segregata	Florida privet	N,C,S	5-20 ft	S	H	H
Iva frutescens	Marsh elder	N,C,S	3-10 ft	S	L	M
Myrica cerifera	Southern wax myrtle ST	N,C,S	20 ft	S, PSh, Sh	H	H
Randia aculeata	White indigoberry ST	C,S	6 ft	S, PSh	H	M
Sabal etonia	Scrub palmetto	C,S	6-10 ft	S, PSh	H	H
Serenoa repens	Saw palmetto ST *	N,C,S	10 ft	S, PSh	H	H
Yucca aloifolia	Spanish bayonet ST *	N,C,S	12-15 ft	S	M	M

COASTAL STRAND TREES

Scientific Name	Common Name	Range	Mature Height	Light Requirement	Wildlife Value Food	Wildlife Value Cover
Small Trees						
Coccoloba diversifolia	Pigeon plum ST	C,S	30 ft	S	H	H
Coccoloba uvifera	Sea grape ST	C,S	15 ft	S	M	H
Ilex vomitoria	Yaupon holly ST	N,C	15 ft	S, PSh	H	H
Pinus clausa	Sand pine ST	N,C,S	35 ft	S	M	M
Quercus myrtifolia	Myrtle oak	N,C,S	35 ft	S	H	H
Ximenia americana	Tallowwood plum ST	S	20-25 ft	S	H	H
Large Trees						
Juniperus silicicola	Southern red cedar ST	N,C,S	40 ft	S, PSh	H	H
Lysiloma latisiliquum	Wild tamarind ST	S	40-50 ft	S	L	H
Pinus palustris	Long leaf pine	N,C,S	100 ft	S	M	M
Quercus virginiana	Live oak ST *	N,C,S	70 ft	S	H	H
Sabal palmetto	Cabbage palm ST *	N,C,S	60 ft	S, PSh	H	H

RANGE:
  N = North Florida, C = Central Florida, S = South Florida
LIGHT REQUIREMENTS:
  S = Sun, Sh = Shade, PSh = Partial Shade

* = Plants characteristic of Coastal Strand
ST = Salt tolerant
WILDLIFE VALUES:
  L = Low, M = Medium, H = High

Sand Scrub Plant Tables

SAND SCRUB GRASSES

Scientific Name	Common Name	Range	Mature Height	Light Requirement	Wildlife Value Food	Cover
Andropogon virginicus	Broomsedge bluestem	N,C,S	6 ft	S, PSh	—	—
Aristida purpurascens	Arrowfeather threeawn	N,C,S	3 ft	S, PSh	—	—
Aristida stricta	Wiregrass	N,C,S	3 ft	S, PSh	—	—
Dichanthelium aciculare	Panicum needleleaf	N,C,S	2 ft	S, PSh	—	—
Eragrotis spectabilis	Purple lovegrass	N,C,S	2 ft	S, PSh	—	—
Sorghastrum secundum	Lopsided indiangrass	N,C,S	6 ft	S, PSh	—	—
Sporobolus junceus	Pinewoods dropseed	N,C,S	3 ft	S, PSh	—	—

SAND SCRUB GRASSLIKES

Scientific Name	Common Name	Range	Mature Height	Light Requirement	Wildlife Value Food	Cover
Carex spp.	Caric sedges	N,C,S	0.5-3 ft	S, PSh, Sh	—	—
Rhynchospora spp.	Beakrush	N,C,S	2 ft	S, PSh	—	—

SAND SCRUB HERBACEOUS

Scientific Name	Common Name	Range	Mature Height	Light Requirement	Wildlife Value Food	Cover
Commelina spp.	Day flower *	N,C,S	2 ft	S, PSh	—	—
Crotonopsis linearis	Rushfloil	N,C,S	0.5-1 ft	S	—	—
Gaillardia pulchella	Blanket flower	N,C,S	1-1.5 ft	S, PSh	—	—
Heterotheca subaxillaris	Camphorweed	N,C,S	2-4 ft	S	—	—
Portulaca pilosa	Portulaca	N,C,S	3-8 ft	S	—	—
Sisyrinchium spp.	Blue-eyed grass	N,C,S	1 ft	S, PSh	—	—
Solidago spp.	Goldenrod	N,C,S	2-4 ft	S, PSh	—	—
Tradescantia spp.	Spiderwort	N,C,S	2 ft	S, PSh	—	—
Veronia spp.	Ironweed	N,C,S	2-4 ft	S, PSh	—	—

SAND SCRUB VINES

Scientific Name	Common Name	Range	Mature Height	Light Requirement	Wildlife Value Food	Cover
Ampelopsis arborea	Peppervine [I]	N,C,S	—	S, PSh	—	—
Centrosema virginianum	Butterfly pea	N,C,S	—	S, PSh	—	—
Gelsemium sempervirens	Yellow jessamine [T]	N,C,S	—	S, PSh	—	—
Vitis spp.	Wild grape *	N,C,S	—	S, PSh, Sh	—	—

RANGE:
   N = North Florida, C = Central Florida, S = South Florida
LIGHT REQUIREMENTS:
   S = Sun, Sh = Shade, PSh = Partial Shade

* = Plants characteristic of Coastal Strand
[T] = Toxic plant   [I] = Irritant plant
WILDLIFE VALUES:
   L = Low, M = Medium, H = High

SAND SCRUB SHRUBS

Scientific Name	Common Name	Range	Mature Height	Light Requirement	Wildlife Value	
					Food	Cover
Small Shrubs						
Hypericum spp.	St. John's wort	N,C,S	3 ft	S, PSh	L	L
Licania michauxii	Gopher apple *	N,C	0.5-1 ft	S, PSh	H	L
Quercus pumila	Runner oak	N,C,S	1-2 ft	S, PSh	H	H
Yucca filamentosa	Bear grass *	N,C,S	2-4 ft	S	M	M
Large Shrubs						
Lyonia lucida	Fetterbush	N,C,S	8 ft	S, PSh	L	H
Sabal etonia	Scrub palmetto	C,S	6-10 ft	S, PSh	H	H
Serenoa repens	Saw palmetto *	N,C,S	10 ft	S, PSh	H	H
Vaccinium arboreum	Sparkleberry	N,C	25 ft	S, PSh	H	H

SAND SCRUB TREES

Scientific Name	Common Name	Range	Mature Height	Light Requirement	Wildlife Value	
					Food	Cover
Small Trees						
Crataegus spp.	Hawthorne	N,C,S	15-20 ft	S, PSh	H	H
Ilex ambigua	Carolina holly	N,C,S	15 ft	S, PSh	H	H
Pinus clausa	Sand pine *	N,C,S	35 ft	S	M	M
Quercus chapmanii	Chapman oak *	N,C,S	20-30 ft	S	H	H
Quercus incana	Bluejack oak *	N,C,S	35 ft	S	H	M
Quercus laevis	Turkey oak *	N,C,S	20-30 ft	S	H	H
Quercus marilandica	Blackjack oak	N	20-30 ft	S	H	H
Quercus myrtifolia	Myrtle oak *	N,C,S	35 ft	S	H	H
Large Trees						
Carya floridana	Scrub hickory *	C,S	50-70 ft	S, PSh	H	M
Carya glabra	Pignut hickory	N,C,S	60 ft	S	H	H
Diospyros virginiana	Common persimmon	N,C,S	30-60 ft	S	H	M
Juniperus silicicola	Southern red cedar	N,C,S	40 ft	S, PSh	H	H
Osmanthus americanus	Wild olive	N,C,S	50-70 ft	S, PSh	H	M
Pinus palustris	Long leaf pine	N,C,S	100 ft	S	M	M
Quercus virginiana	Live oak	N,C,S	70 ft	S	H	H

RANGE:
   N = North Florida, C = Central Florida, S = South Florida
LIGHT REQUIREMENTS:
   S = Sun, Sh = Shade, PSh = Partial Shade

* = Plants characteristic of Coastal Strand
WILDLIFE VALUES:
   L = Low, M = Medium, H = High

Sandhill PlantTables

SANDHILL GRASSES

Scientific Name	Common Name	Range	Mature Height	Light Requirement	Wildlife Value Food	Cover
Andropogon virginicus	Broomsedge bluestem	N,C,S	6 ft	S, PSh	—	—
Aristida purpurascens	Arrowfeather threeawn	N,C,S	3 ft	S, PSh	—	—
Aristida stricta	Wiregrass *	N,C,S	3 ft	S, PSh	—	—
Dichanthelium aciculare	Panicum needleleaf	N,C,S	2 ft	S, PSh	—	—
Eragrostis elliottii	Elliott lovegrass	N,C,S	3 ft	S, PSh	—	—
Eustachys petraea	Stiffleaf chloris	N,C,S	3 ft	S	—	—
Sorghastrum secundum	Lopsided indiangrass	N,C,S	6 ft	S, PSh	—	—
Sporobolus junceus	Pinewoods dropseed *	N,C,S	3 ft	S, PSh	—	—

SANDHILL HERBACEOUS

Scientific Name	Common Name	Range	Mature Height	Light Requirement	Wildlife Value Food	Cover
Asclepias tuberosa	Butterfly weed [T]	N,C,S	2 ft	S, PSh	—	—
Commelina spp.	Day flower	N,C,S	2 ft	S, PSh	—	—
Coreopsis spp.	Tickseed	N,C,S	1-3 ft	S, PSh, Sh	—	—
Elephantopus spp.	Elephant's foot	N,C,S	2 ft	S, PSh	—	—
Gaillardia pulchella	Blanket flower	N,C,S	1-1.5 ft	S, PSh	—	—
Monarda punctata	Beebalm (Horsemint)	N,C,S	1-3 ft	S, PSh	—	—
Portulaca pilosa	Portulaca	N,C,S	3-8 ft	S	—	—
Pteridum aquilinum	Bracken fern * [T]	N,C,S	1-3 ft	S, PSh, Sh	—	—
Rudbeckia hirta	Black eyed Susan [I]	N,C,S	1-3 ft	S, PSh	—	—
Sisyrinchium spp.	Blue-eyed grass	N,C,S	1 ft	S, PSh	—	—
Tradescantia spp.	Spiderwort	N,C,S	2 ft	S, PSh	—	—
Veronia spp.	Ironweed	N,C,S	2-4 ft	S, PSh	—	—

SANDHILL VINES

Scientific Name	Common Name	Range	Mature Height	Light Requirement	Wildlife Value Food	Cover
Ampelopsis arborea	Peppervine [I]	N,C,S	—	S, PSh	—	—
Centrosema virginianum	Butterfly pea *	N,C,S	—	S, PSh	—	—
Passiflora edulis	Maypop (Passion flower)	N,C,S	—	S, PSh	—	—
Rhynchosia spp.	Rhynchosia	N,C,S	—	S, PSh	—	—
Rubus argutus	Blackberry	N,C,S	—	S, PSh	—	—
Vitis spp.	Wild grape	N,C,S	—	S, PSh, Sh	—	—

RANGE:
  N = North Florida, C = Central Florida, S = South Florida
LIGHT REQUIREMENTS:
  S = Sun, Sh = Shade, PSh = Partial Shade

* = Plants characteristic of Coastal Strand
[T] = Toxic plant   [I] = Irritant plant
WILDLIFE VALUES:
  L = Low, M = Medium, H = High

SANDHILL SHRUBS

Scientific Name	Common Name	Range	Mature Height	Light Requirement	Wildlife Value Food	Cover
Small Shrubs						
Asimina reticulata	Pawpaw	N,C,S	3 ft	S, PSh	H	M
Callicarpa americana	American beautyberry	N,C,S	6 ft	S, PSh	H	M
Licania michauxii	Gopher apple *	N,C	0.5-1 ft	S, PSh	H	L
Quercus pumilla	Runner oak	N,C,S	1-2 ft	S, PSh	H	H
Yucca filamentosa	Bear grass	N,C,S	2-4 ft	S	M	M
Zamia spp.	Coontie	N,C,S	3 ft	S, PSh	L	L
Large Shrubs						
Castanea alnifolia	Chinkapin	N	25 ft	S, PSh, Sh	H	H
Chionanthus pygmaeus	Pygmy fringe tree	C,S	15 ft	S, PSh, Sh	M	H
Erythrina herbacea	Coralbean ᵀ	N,C,S	8 ft	S, PSh	H	M
Ilex ambigua	Carolina holly	N,C,S	15 ft	S, PSh	H	H
Ilex vomitoria	Yaupon holly	N,C	15 ft	S, PSh	H	H
Serenoa repens	Saw palmetto	N,C,S	10 ft	S, PSh	H	H
Vaccinium arboreum	Sparkleberry	N,C	25 ft	S, PSh	H	H
Viburnum rufidulum	Rusty blackhaw	N	15 ft	S, PSh	H	H

SANDHILL TREES

Scientific Name	Common Name	Range	Mature Height	Light Requirement	Wildlife Value Food	Cover
Small Trees						
Crataegus spp.	Hawthorne	N,C,S	15-20 ft	S, PSh	H	H
Ilex ambigua	Carolina holly	N,C,S	15 ft	S, PSh	H	H
Prunus americana	American plum ᵀ	N,C,S	20 ft	S, PSh	H	H
Prunus angustifolia	Chickasaw plum ᵀ	N,C	25 ft	S, PSh	H	H
Quercus chapmanii	Chapman oak	N,C,S	20-30 ft	S	H	H
Quercus incana	Bluejack oak	N,C,S	35 ft	S	H	M
Quercus laevis	Turkey oak *	N,C,S	20-30 ft	S	H	H
Quercus marilandica	Blackjack oak	N	20-30 ft	S	H	H
Quercus myrtifolia	Myrtle oak	N,C,S	35 ft	S	H	H
Large Trees						
Ilex opaca	American holly	N,C,S	30-50 ft	S.PSh	H	H
Juniperus silicicola	Southern red cedar	N,C,S	40 ft	S, PSh	H	H
Pinus clausa	Sand pine	N,C,S	35 ft	S	M	M
Pinus elliottii	Slash pine	N,C,S	80 ft	S	M	M
Pinus palustris	Longleaf pine *	N,C,S	100 ft	S	M	M
Quercus virginiana	Live oak	N,C,S	70 ft	S	H	H

RANGE:
  N = North Florida, C = Central Florida, S = South Florida
LIGHT REQUIREMENTS:
  S = Sun, Sh = Shade, PSh = Partial Shade

* = Plants characteristic of Coastal Strand
ᵀ = Toxic plant
WILDLIFE VALUES:
  L = Low, M = Medium, H = High

Hardwood Hammock Plant Tables

HARDWOOD HAMMOCK GRASSES

Scientific Name	Common Name	Range	Mature Height	Light Requirement	Wildlife Value Food	Wildlife Value Cover
Andropogon virginicus	Broomsedge bluestem	N,C,S	6 ft	S, PSh	—	—
Aristida spp.	Threeawn	N,C,S	3 ft	S, PSh	—	—
Aristida stricta	Wiregrass	N,C,S	3 ft	S, PSh	—	—
Eragrostis elliottii	Elliott lovegrass	N,C,S	3 ft	S, PSh	—	—
Eustachys glauca	Saltmarsh chloris	N,C,S	3 ft	S	—	—
Eustachys petraea	Stiffleaf chloris	N,C,S	3 ft	S	—	—
Panicum hemitomon	Maidencane	N,C,S	6 ft	S, PSh	—	—
Panicum spp.	Low panicum *	S	3 ft	S, PSh	—	—
Paspalum conjugatum	Sour paspalum *	S	3 ft	S, PSh	—	—
Sorghastrum secundum	Lopsided indiangrass	N,C,S	6 ft	S, PSh	—	—
Tripsacum dactyloides	Eastern gamagrass	C,S	6 ft	S, PSh	—	—

HARDWOOD HAMMOCK GRASSLIKES

Scientific Name	Common Name	Range	Mature Height	Light Requirement	Wildlife Value Food	Wildlife Value Cover
Carex spp.	Caric sedges	N,C,S	0.5-3 ft	S, PSh, Sh	—	—
Eleocharis spp.	Spikerush	N,C,S	0.5-2 ft	S, PSh, Sh	—	—
Rhynchospora spp.	Beakrush	N,C,S	2 ft	S, PSh	—	—

HARDWOOD HAMMOCK HERBACEOUS

Scientific Name	Common Name	Range	Mature Height	Light Requirement	Wildlife Value Food	Wildlife Value Cover
Arisaema dracontium	Green dragon	N	1 ft	PSh, Sh	—	—
Arisaema triphyllum	Jack-in-the-pulpit [I]	N,C	1 ft	PSh, Sh	—	—
Asclepias spp.	Milkweed [T]	N,C,S	2 ft	S, PSh	—	—
Asclepias tuberosa	Butterfly weed [T]	N,C,S	2 ft	S, PSh	—	—
Aster dumosus	Bush aster	N,C,S	1-4 ft	S, PSh	—	—
Athyrium filix-femina	Lady fern	C,S	2-3 ft	PSh, Sh	—	—
Baptisia spp.	Wild indigo	N,C,S	1-2 ft	S, PSh	—	—
Commelina spp.	Day flower	N,C,S	2 ft	S, PSh	—	—
Conoclinium coelestinum	Mistflower	N,C	1-2 ft	PSh	—	—
Cyperus odoratus	Flatsedges	N,C,S	2 ft	S, PSh	—	—
Dryopteris ludoviciani	Southern shieldfern	N,C	1-3 ft	PSh, Sh	—	—
Elephantopus spp.	Elephant's foot	N,C,S	2 ft	S, PSh	—	—
Ipomopsis rubra	Standing cypress	N,C,S	2-3 ft	S, PSh	—	—
Mitchella repens	Partridge berry	N,C,S	0.5 ft	PSh, Sh	—	—
Monarda punctata	Beebalm (Horsemint) *	N,C,S	1-3 ft	S, PSh	—	—
Nephrolepis biserrata	Boston fern *	S	3 ft	PSh, Sh	—	—
Nephrolepis exallata	Sword fern	S	3 ft	PSh, Sh	—	—
Osmunda cinnamomea	Cinnamon fern	N,C,S	3-4 ft	PSh, Sh	—	—
Osmunda regalis	Royal fern	N,C,S	3-4 ft	PSh, Sh	—	—
Phlebodium aureum	Golden serpent fern *	S	3 ft	PSh, Sh	—	—

(continued on next page)

RANGE:
    N = North Florida, C = Central Florida, S = South Florida
LIGHT REQUIREMENTS:
    S = Sun, Sh = Shade, PSh = Partial Shade

* = Plants characteristic of Coastal Strand
[T] = Toxic plant [I] = Irritant plant
WILDLIFE VALUES:
    L = Low, M = Medium, H = High

(Hardwood Hammock Herbaceous continued)

Scientific Name	Common Name	Range	Mature Height	Light Requirement	Wildlife Value	
					Food	Cover
Polypodium polypodioides	Resurrection fern *	S	3 ft	PSh, Sh	—	—
Pteridum aquilinum	Bracken fern * [T]	N,C,S	1-3 ft	S, PSh, Sh	—	—
Rudbeckia hirta	Black-eyed Susan [I]	N,C,S	1-3 ft	S, PSh	—	—
Saururus cernuus	Lizard's tail	N,C,S	2 ft	PSh, Sh	—	—
Tillandsia fasciculata	Stiff-leaved wild pine *	S	3 ft	S, PSh, Sh	—	—
Woodwardia areolata	Chain fern	N,C,S	3 ft	PSh, Sh	—	—
Zephyranthes spp.	Atamasca lily [T]	N,C,S	1 ft	S, PSh	—	—

HARDWOOD HAMMOCK VINES

Scientific Name	Common Name	Range	Mature Height	Light Requirement	Wildlife Value	
					Food	Cover
Ampelopsis arborea	Peppervine [I]	N,C,S	—	S, PSh	—	—
Bignonia carpreolata	Crossvine *	N,C	—	S, PSh	—	—
Campsis radicans	Trumpet creeper [I]	N,C,S	—	S, PSh	—	—
Centrosema virginianum	Butterfly pea	N,C,S	—	S, PSh	—	—
Decumaria barbara	Climbing hydrangea	N,C	—	PSh		
Gelsemium sempervirens	Yellow jessamine [T]	N,C,S	—	S, PSh	—	—
Mimosa strigillosa	Sensitive vine	N,C	—	S, PSh	—	—
Parthenocissus quinquefolia	Virginia creeper * [T]	N,C,S	—	S, PSh	—	—
Passiflora edulis	Maypop (Passion flower)	N,C,S	—	S, PSh	—	—
Rubus argutus	Blackberry	N,C,S	—	S, PSh	—	—
Vitis spp.	Wild grape *	N,C,S	—	S, PSh, Sh	—	—

HARDWOOD HAMMOCK SHRUBS

Scientific Name	Common Name	Range	Mature Height	Light Requirement	Wildlife Value	
					Food	Cover
Small Shrubs						
Amorpha fruticosa	Indigo-bush	N	3-6 ft	PSh, Sh	H	M
Callicarpa americana	American beautyberry *	N,C,S	6 ft	S, PSh	H	M
Chiococca alba	Snowberry *	C,S	6-9 ft	S, PSh	H	H
Euonymus americanus	Strawberry bush	N	5 ft	PSh	M	M
Hypericum spp.	St. John's wort	N,C,S	3 ft	S, PSh	L	L
Itea virginica	Sweetspire	N,C,	4-6 ft	S, PSh	L	L
Psychotria nervosa	Wild coffee (* in S Fl)	C,S	2 ft	PSh Sh	H	H
Randia aculeata	White indigoberry (* in S Fl)	C,S	6 ft	S, PSh	H	M
Rhapidophyllum hystrix	Needle palm	N,C	6 ft	PSh	M	M
Yucca filamentosa	Bear grass	N,C,S	2-4 ft	S	M	M
Zamia spp.	Coontie	N,C,S	3 ft	S, PSh	L	L
Large Shrubs						
Amyris elemifera	Torchwood *	S	15 ft	PSh,Sh	H	M
Ardisia escallonoides	Marlberry *	S	20 ft	PSh,Sh	H	H

(continued on next page)

RANGE:
    N = North Florida, C = Central Florida, S = South Florida
LIGHT REQUIREMENTS:
    S = Sun, Sh = Shade, PSh = Partial Shade

* = Plants characteristic of Coastal Strand
[T] = Toxic plant   [I] = Irritant plant
WILDLIFE VALUES:
    L = Low, M = Medium, H = High

(Hardwood Hammock Shrubs continued)

Scientific Name	Common Name	Range	Mature Height	Light Requirement	Wildlife Value Food	Wildlife Value Cover
Large Shrubs continued						
Chrysobalanus icaco	Coco-plum *	S	15 ft	S	H	H
Coccoloba uvifera	Sea grape (* in S Fl)	C,S	15 ft	S	M	H
Erythrina herbacea	Coralbean ᵀ	N,C,S	8 ft	S, PSh	H	M
Eugenia foetida	Span. stopper (* in S Fl)	C,S	15 ft	S,PSh	H	H
Hamamelis virginiana	Witch-hazel	N	20-30 ft	S, PSh, Sh	L	H
Ilex ambigua	Carolina holly	N,C,S	15 ft	S, PSh	H	H
Ilex decidua	Possumhaw	N,C	15 ft	S, PSh	H	H
Ilex vomitoria	Yaupon holly	N,C	15 ft	S, PSh, Sh	H	H
Jacquinia keyensis	Joewood *	S	20 ft	PSh	H	H
Mastichodendron foetidissimum	Mastic *	S	15 ft	PSh	H	H
Myrica cerifera	Southern wax myrtle *	N,C,S	20 ft	S, PSh, Sh	H	H
Rhamnus caroliniana	Carolina buckthorn	N,C	20-30 ft	S, PSh	H	L
Rhododendron serrulatum	Hammocksweet azalea	N	16 ft	S, PSh	M	M
Sabal minor	Dwarf palmetto	N,C,S	8 ft	S, PSh	M	M
Serenoa repens	Saw palmetto	N,C,S	10 ft	S, PSh	H	H
Vaccinium arboreum	Sparkleberry *	N,C	25 ft	S, PSh	H	H
Viburnum dentatum	Arrowwood *	N,C	10 ft	S, PSh	H	H
Viburnum obovatum	Walter viburnum	N,C,S	25 ft	S, PSh	H	H
Viburnum rufidulum	Rusty blackhaw	N	15 ft	S, PSh	H	H

HARDWOOD HAMMOCK TREES

Scientific Name	Common Name	Range	Mature Height	Light Requirement	Wildlife Value Food	Wildlife Value Cover
Small Trees						
Acer saccharum	Southern sugar maple	N,	30 ft	S	H	H
Aesculus pavia	Red buckeye ᵀ	N,C	25 ft	PSh	H	H
Aralia spinosa	Devil's walking stick ᴵ	N,C,S	35 ft	S, PSh	M	H
Chionanthus virginicus	Fringetree	N,C,S	25 ft	S, PSh	M	H
Cornus florida	Flowering dogwood	N,C	30 ft	PSh	H	M
Drypetes laterifolia	Guiana plum	S	25 ft	PSh	L	L
Eugenia axillaris	White stopper	C,S	20-30 ft	S	H	H
Guapira discolor	Blolly *	S	25 ft	S,PSh	H	H
Guettarda elliptica	Velvetseed *	S	30 ft	S,PSh	H	H
Krugiodendron ferreum	Black ironwood *	S	30 ft	S,PSh	M	H
Nectandra coriacea	Lancewood *	S	30 ft	S,PSh	H	M
Prunus americana	American plum ᵀ	N,C,S	20 ft	S, PSh	H	H
Prunus angustifolia	Chickasaw plum ᵀ	N,C	25 ft	S, PSh	H	H
Prunus umbellata	Flatwoods plum ᵀ	N,C,S	20-35 ft	S	H	H
Quercus incana	Bluejack oak	N,C,S	35 ft	S	H	M
Quercus laevis	Turkey oak	N,C,S	20-30 ft	S	H	H
Sambucus canadensis	Elderberry	N,C,S	20 ft	S, PSh	H	H
Sapindus saponaria	Wingleaf soapberry	N,C,S	30 ft	PSh	H	M

(continued on next page)

RANGE:
  N = North Florida, C = Central Florida, S = South Florida
LIGHT REQUIREMENTS:
  S = Sun, Sh = Shade, PSh = Partial Shade

* = Plants characteristic of Coastal Strand
ᵀ = Toxic plant   ᴵ = Irritant plant
WILDLIFE VALUES:
  L = Low, M = Medium, H = High

(Hardwood Hammock Trees continued)

Scientific Name	Common Name	Range	Mature Height	Light Requirement	Wildlife Value Food	Wildlife Value Cover
Large Trees						
Acer negundo	Box elder	N,C	60 ft	S, PSh	H	H
Acer rubrum	Red maple	N,C,S	40 ft	S	H	H
Bursera simaruba	Gumbo limbo *	S	50 ft	S	M	M
Carya glabra	Pignut hickory *	N,C,S	60 ft	S	H	H
Carya tomentosa	Mockernut hickory	N,C	70 ft	S, PSh	H	H
Cercis canadensis	Redbud	N,C	40 ft	S, PSh	H	M
Chrysophyllum oliviforme	Satinleaf *	S	40 ft	S	H	L
Coccoloba diversifolia	Pigeon plum *	C,S	30 ft	S	H	H
Conocarpus erecta	Buttonwood *	S	60 ft	S	H	H
Diospyros virginiana	Common persimmon	N,C,S	30-60 ft	S	H	M
Exothea paniculata	Inkwood	C,S	50 ft	S	H	H
Fagus grandifolia	American beech *	N	60-80 ft	S	H	H
Ficus aurea	Strangler fig	C,S	50-60 ft	S	H	H
Hypelate trifoliata	Hypelate or Ironwood *	S	30-40 ft	PSh	H	H
Ilex cassine	Dahoon holly	N,C,S	40 ft	S, PSh	H	H
Ilex opaca	American holly *	N,C,S	30-50 ft	S, PSh	H	H
Juniperus silicicola	Southern red cedar	N,C,S	40 ft	S, PSh	H	H
Liquidambar styraciflua	Sweetgum	N,C,S	85 ft	S	L	H
Liriodendron tulipifera	Yellow poplar	N,C	100-200 ft	S	L	H
Lysiloma bahamense	Wild tamarind *	S	40-50 ft	S	L	H
Magnolia grandiflora	Southern magnolia	N,C,S	50	S, PSh	H	H
Osmanthus americanus	Wild olive	N,C,S	50-70 ft	S, PSh	H	M
Ostrya virginiana	Eastern hophornbean	N	40 ft	PSh, Sh	M	H
Persea borbonia	Redbay	N,C,S	50 ft	S, PSh	H	H
Pinus elliottii	Slash pine	N,C,S	80 ft	S	M	M
Pinus glabra	Spruce pine	N,C	90 ft	S, PSh	M	M
Pinus palustris	Longleaf pine	N,C,S	100 ft	S	M	M
Pinus serotina	Pond pine	N,C	40-70 ft	S	M	M
Pinus taeda	Loblolly pine [T]	N,C	80 ft	S	M	M
Prunus caroliniana	Carolina laurelcherry [T]	N,C,S	30-40 ft	S	H	H
Prunus serotina	Black cherry [T]	N,C	50-60 ft	S	H	H
Quercus alba	White oak	N	80-150 ft	S	H	H
Quercus falcata	Southern red oak	N,C	70-80 ft	S	H	H
Quercus laurifolia	Laurel oak *	N,C,S	75 ft	S, PSh	H	H
Quercus michauxii	Swamp chestnut oak	N,C	75 ft	S, PSh	H	H
Quercus virginiana	Live oak *	N,C,S	70 ft	S	H	H
Rhamnus caroliniana	Carolina buckthorn	N,C	20-30 ft	S, PSh	H	L
Sabal palmetto	Cabbage palm (* in S Fl)	N,C,S	60 ft	S, PSh	H	H
Taxoidum distchum	Bald cypress	N,C,S	100 ft	S, PSh	L	M
Trema micrantha	Florida trema *	S	40 ft	S	H	L
Ulmus alata	Winged elm	N,C,S	50 ft	S, PSh	M	H
Ulmus americana	American elm	N,C,S	60 ft	S	M	H
Zanthoxylum	Hercules-club clava-herculis	N,C,S	30-40 ft	S, PSh	M	M
Thrinax radiata	Thatchpalm	S	20 ft	S, PSh	H	H
Zanthoxylum fagara	Wild lime	C,S	25-30 ft	S, PSh	H	M

RANGE:
  N = North Florida, C = Central Florida, S = South Florida
LIGHT REQUIREMENTS:
  S = Sun, Sh = Shade, PSh = Partial Shade

* = Plants characteristic of Coastal Strand
[T] = Toxic plant
WILDLIFE VALUES:
  L = Low, M = Medium, H = High

Flatwood Plant Tables

FLATWOOD GRASSES

Scientific Name	Common Name	Range	Mature Height	Light Requirement	Wildlife Value Food	Wildlife Value Cover
Andropogon virginicus	Broomsedge bluestem	N,C,S	6 ft	S, PSh	—	—
Aristida purpurascens	Arrowfeather threeawn	N,C,S	3 ft	S, PSh	—	—
Aristida stricta	Wiregrass *	N,C,S	3 ft	S, PSh	—	—
Dichanthelium aciculare	Panicum needleleaf	N,C,S	2 ft	S. PSh	—	—
Eragrostis elliottii	Elliott lovegrass	N,C,S	3 ft	S, PSh	—	—
Panicum hemitomon	Maidencane	N,C,S	6 ft	S, PSh	—	—
Sorghastrum secundum	Lopsided indiangrass *	N,C,S	6 ft	S, PSh	—	—
Sporobolus junceus	Pinewoods dropseed	N,C,S	3 ft	S. PSh	—	—

FLATWOOD GRASSLIKES

Scientific Name	Common Name	Range	Mature Height	Light Requirement	Wildlife Value Food	Wildlife Value Cover
Carex spp.	Caric sedges	N,C,S	0.5-3 ft	S, PSh, Sh	—	—
Dichromena colorata	Star rush	N,C,S	2 ft	S. PSh	—	—
Dichromena floridensis	White-top rush	N,C,S	2 ft	S, PSh	—	—
Eleocharis spp.	Spikerush	N,C,S	0.5-2 ft	S, PSh, Sh	—	—
Fuirena scirpoidea	Umbrella grass	N,C,S	2 ft	S, PSh	—	—
Rhynchospora spp.	Beakrush	N,C,S	2 ft	S, PSh	—	—

FLATWOOD HERBACEOUS

Scientific Name	Common Name	Range	Mature Height	Light Requirement	Wildlife Value Food	Wildlife Value Cover
Agalinis spp.	Gerardia	N,C,S	2 ft	S. PSh	—	—
Amorpha crenulata	Lead plant	N,C	2 ft	S, PSh	—	—
Asclepias spp.	Milkweed T	N,C,S	2 ft	S, PSh	—	—
Carphephorus corymbosus	Carphephorus (Chaffhead)	N,C,S	2 ft	S, PSh	—	—
Conoclinium coelestinum	Mistflower	N,C	1-2 ft	PSh	—	—
Coreopsis spp.	Tickseed	N,C,S	1-3 ft	S, PSh, Sh	—	—
Cyperus odoratus	Flatsedges	N,C,S	2 ft	S, PSh	—	—
Elephantopus spp.	Elephant's foot	N,C,S	2 ft	S, PSh	—	—
Eriocaulon spp.	Pipewort or hatpin	N,C,S	2 ft	S, PSh	—	—
Hibiscus moscheutos	Rose mallow	N,C,S	2 ft	S, PSh	—	—
Hymenocallis spp.	Spider lily	N,C,S	2 ft	S, PSh	—	—
Iris virginica	Blue flag iris	N,C,S	4 ft	PSh	—	—
Lachnocaulon spp.	Bog button	N,C,S	2 ft	S, PSh	—	—
Liatris chapmanii	Blazing star	N,C,S	2 ft	S, PSh	—	—
Lilium catesbaei	Catesby's lily (Pine lily)	N,C,S	2 ft	S, PSh	—	—
Nolina atopocarpa	Florida bear grass	N,C	2 ft	S, PSh	—	—
Osmunda cinnamomea	Cinnamon fern	N,C,S	3-4 ft	PSh, Sh	—	—
Osmunda regalis	Royal fern	N,C,S	3-4 ft	PSh, Sh	—	—

(continued on next page)

RANGE:
    N = North Florida, C = Central Florida, S = South Florida
LIGHT REQUIREMENTS:
    S = Sun, Sh = Shade, PSh = Partial Shade

* = Plants characteristic of Coastal Strand
T = Toxic plant
WILDLIFE VALUES:
    L = Low, M = Medium, H = High

Landscaping for Florida's Wildlife

(Flatwood Herbaceous continued)

Scientific Name	Common Name	Range	Mature Height	Light Requirement	Wildlife Value Food	Cover
Pteridum aquilinum	Bracken fern *	N,C,S	1-3 ft	S, PSh, Sh	—	—
Rhexia spp.	Knotweed	N,C,S	2 ft	S, PSh	—	—
Rudbeckia spp.	Coneflower	N,C,S	4 ft	S, PSh	—	—
Salvia coccinea	Tropical sage	N,C,S	2 ft	S, PSh	—	—
Sisyrinchium spp.	Blue-eyed grass	N,C,S	1 ft	S, PSh	—	—
Solidago spp.	Goldenrod	N,C,S	2-4 ft	S, PSh	—	—
Tradescantia spp.	Spiderwort	N,C,S	2 ft	S, PSh	—	—
Veronia spp.	Ironweed	N,C,S	2-4 ft	S, PSh	—	—
Woodwardia areolata	Chain fern	N,C,S	3 ft	PSh, Sh	—	—
Xyris spp.	Yellow-eyed grass	N,C,S	2 ft	S, PSh	—	—
Zephyranthes spp.	Atamasca lily [T]	N,C,S	1 ft	S, PSh	—	—

FLATWOOD VINES

Scientific Name	Common Name	Range	Mature Height	Light Requirement	Wildlife Value Food	Cover
Ampelopsis arborea	Peppervine [I]	N,C,S	—	S, PSh	—	—
Campsis radicans	Trumpet creeper [I]	N,C,S	—	S, PSh	—	—
Centrosema virginianum	Butterfly pea	N,C,S	—	S, PSh	—	—
Gelsemium sempervirens	Yellow jessamine [T]	N,C,S	—	S, PSh	—	—
Mimosa strigillosa	Sensitive vine	N,C	—	S, PSh	—	—
Passiflora edulis	Maypop (Passion flower)	N,C,S	—	S, PSh	—	—
Rhynchosia spp.	Rhynchosia	N,C,S	—	S. PSh	—	—
Rubus argutus	Blackberry *	N,C,S	—	S, PSh	—	—
Vitis spp.	Wild grape	N,C,S	—	S, PSh, Sh	—	—

FLATWOOD SHRUBS

Scientific Name	Common Name	Range	Mature Height	Light Requirement	Wildlife Value Food	Cover
Small Shrubs						
Hypericum spp.	St. John's wort	N,C,S	3 ft	S, PSh	L	L
Itea virginica	Sweetspire	N,C	4-6 ft	S, PSh	L	L
Licania michauxii	Gopher apple	N,C	0.5-1 ft	S, PSh	H	L
Quercus pumila	Runner oak	N,C,S	1-2 ft	S, PSh	H	H
Zamia spp.	Coontie	N,C,S	3 ft	S, PSh	L	L
Large Shrubs						
Aronia arbutifolia	Red chokeberry	N,C	8 ft	S. PSh	H	H
Befaria racemosa	Tarflower	N,C,S	8 ft	S. PSh	M	H
Clethra alnifolia	Summersweet clethra	N	10 ft	S, PSh	M	M
Erythrina herbacea	Coralbean [T]	N,C,S	8 ft	S, PSh	H	M
Ilex coriacea	Giant gallberry	N	15 ft	S, PSh, Sh	H	M

(continued on next page)

RANGE:
    N = North Florida, C = Central Florida, S = South Florida
LIGHT REQUIREMENTS:
    S = Sun, Sh = Shade, PSh = Partial Shade

* = Plants characteristic of Coastal Strand
[T] = Toxic plant   [I] = Irritant plant
WILDLIFE VALUES:
    L = Low, M = Medium, H = High

(Flatwood Herbaceous continued)

Scientific Name	Common Name	Range	Mature Height	Light Requirement	Wildlife Value Food	Wildlife Value Cover
(Large Shrubs continued)						
Ilex glabra	Common gallberry *	N,C,S	8 ft	S, PSh	H	H
Ilex vomitoria	Yaupon holly	N,C	15 ft	S, PSh, Sh	H	H
Lyonia ferruginea	Staggerbush	C,S	30 ft	S, PSh	L	H
Lyonia lucida	Fetterbush	N,C,S	8 ft	S, PSh	L	H
Myrica cerifera	Southern wax myrtle *	N,C,S	20 ft	S, PSh, Sh	H	H
Serenoa repens	Saw palmetto *	N,C,S	10 ft	S, PSh	H	H
Vaccinium arboreum	Sparkleberry	N,C	25 ft	S, PSh	H	H
Sambucus canadensis	Elderberry	N,C,S	20 ft	S, PSh	H	H

FLATWOOD TREES

Scientific Name	Common Name	Range	Mature Height	Light Requirement	Wildlife Value Food	Wildlife Value Cover
Small Trees						
Aralia spinosa	Devil's walking stick [I]	N,C,S	35 ft	S, PSh	M	H
Chionanthus virginicus	Fringetree	N,C,S	25 ft	S, PSh	M	H
Crataegus spp.	Hawthorne	N,C,S	15-20 ft	S, PSh	H	H
Prunus umbellata	Flatwoods plum [T]	N,C,S	20-35 ft	S	H	H
Large Trees						
Carya tomentosa	Mockernut hickory *	N,C	70 ft	S, PSh	H	H
Diospyros virginiana	Common persimmon	N,C,S	30-60 ft	S	H	M
Ilex cassine	Dahoon holly	N,C,S	40 ft	S, PSh	H	H
Ilex opaca	American holly	N,C,S	30-50 ft	S, PSh	H	H
Pinus elliottii	Slash pine *	N,C,S	80 ft	S	M	M
Pinus palustris	Longleaf pine	N,C,S	100 ft	S	M	M
Pinus serotina	Pond pine	N,C	40-70 ft	S	M	M
Pinus taeda	Loblolly pine [T]	N,C	80 ft	S	M	M
Quercus virginiana	Live oak	N,C,S	70 ft	S	H	H
Sabal palmetto	Cabbage palm	N,C,S	60 ft	S, PSh	H	H

RANGE:
   N = North Florida, C = Central Florida, S = South Florida
LIGHT REQUIREMENTS:
   S = Sun, Sh = Shade, PSh = Partial Shade
* = Plants characteristic of Coastal Strand

[T] = Toxic plant   [I] = Irritant plant
WILDLIFE VALUES:
   L = Low, M = Medium, H = High

Swamp Plant Tables

SWAMP GRASSES

Scientific Name	Common Name	Range	Mature Height	Light Requirement	Wildlife Value	
					Food	Cover
Andropogon capillipes	Chalky bluestem	N,C,S	6 ft	S, PSh	—	—
Eustachys glauca	Saltmarsh chloris	N,C,S	3 ft	S	—	—
Panicum hemitomon	Maidencane *	N,C,S	6 ft	S, PSh	—	—
Phragmites australis	Common reed	N,C,S	6 ft	S, PSh	—	—
Tripsacum dactyloides	Eastern gamagrass	C,S	6 ft	S, PSh	—	—
Zizaniopsis miliacea	Giant cutgrass	C,S	10 ft	S, PSh	—	—

SWAMP GRASSLIKES

Scientific Name	Common Name	Range	Mature Height	Light Requirement	Wildlife Value	
					Food	Cover
Carex spp.	Caric sedges	N,C,S	0.5-3 ft	S, PSh, Sh	—	—
Dichromena floridensis	White-top rush	N,C,S	2 ft	S, PSh	—	—
Eleocharis spp.	Spikerush *	N,C,S	0.5-2 ft	S, PSh, Sh	—	—
Fuirena scirpoidea	Umbrella grass	N,C,S	2 ft	S, PSh	—	—
Rhynchospora spp.	Beakrush	N,C,S	2 ft	S, PSh	—	—
Scirpus cyperinus	Giant cutgrass	N,C,S	3-6 ft	S, PSh	—	—

SWAMP HERBACEOUS

Scientific Name	Common Name	Range	Mature Height	Light Requirement	Wildlife Value	
					Food	Cover
Canna flaccida	Golden canna	N,C,S	2 ft	S, PSh	—	—
Commelina spp.	Day flower	N,C,S	2 ft	S, PSh	—	—
Coreopsis spp.	Tickseed [S]	N,C,S	1-3 ft	S, PSh, Sh	—	—
Crinum americanum	Swamp lily [S]	N,C,S	2 ft	S, PSh, Sh	—	—
Cyperus odoratus	Flatsedges	N,C,S	2 ft	S, PSh	—	—
Hymenocallis spp.	Spider lily	N,C,S	2 ft	S, PSh	—	—
Hypoxis spp.	Yellow star grass	N,C,S	2 ft	S, PSh	—	—
Iris spp.	Flag iris	N,C,S	4 ft	PSh	—	—
Lobelia cardinalis	Cardinal flower [S]	N,C,S	2-6 ft	S, PSh	—	—
Nuphar luteum	Spatterdock [D]	N,C,S	1 ft	S, PSh	—	—
Nymphaea mexicana	Yellow water-lily [D]	N,C,S	1 ft	S, PSh	—	—
Nymphaea odorata	Fragrant water-lily [D]	N,C,S	1 ft	S, PSh	—	—
Nymphoides aquatica	Floating heart [D]	N,C,S	1 ft	S, PSh	—	—
Orontium aquaticum	Golden club [S]	N,C	0.5-1 ft	S, PSh	—	—
Osmunda cinnomomea	Cinnamon fern *	N,C,S	3-4 ft	PSh, Sh	—	—
Osmunda regalis	Royal fern *	N,C,S	3-4 ft	PSh, Sh	—	—
Peltandra virginica	Arrow arum [S]	N,C,S	2 ft	S	—	—
Pontedaria cordata	Pickerelweed [S]	N,C,S	4 ft	S		
Rudbeckia spp.	Coneflower	N,C,S	4 ft	S, PSh		
Saggitaria spp.	Arrowhead [S]	N,C,S	2 ft	S, PSh		
Saururus cernuus	Lizard's tail	N,C,S	2 ft	PSh, Sh		
Veronia spp.	Ironweed	N,C,S	2-4 ft	S, PSh		
Woodwardia areolata	Chain fern	N,C,S	3 ft	Psh, Sh		

RANGE:
  N = North Florida, C = Central Florida, S = South Florida
LIGHT REQUIREMENTS:
  S = Sun, Sh = Shade, PSh = Partial Shade
* = Plants characteristic of Coastal Strand

[S] = Example of plants that can be planted in shallow water (< 1 foot deep)
[D] = Example of plants that can be planted in deep water (1 to 4 feet deep)
WILDLIFE VALUES:
  L = Low, M = Medium, H = High

SWAMP VINES

Scientific Name	Common Name	Range	Mature Height	Light Requirement	Wildlife Value	
					Food	Cover
Ampelopsis arborea	Peppervine [I]	N,C,S	—	S, PSh	—	—
Campsis radicans	Trumpet creeper [I]	N,C,S	—	S, PSh	—	—
Decumaria barbara	Climbing hydrangea	N,C	—	PSh	—	—
Gelsemium sempervirens	Yellow jessamine [T]	N,C,S	—	S, PSh	—	—
Parthenocissus quinquefolia	Virginia creeper [T]	N,C,S	—	S, PSh	—	—
Smilax laurifolia	Laurel greenbrier *	N,C,S	—	S, PSh	—	—
Smilax walteri	Coral greenbrier	N,C,S	—	S, PSh	—	—
Vitis spp.	Wild grape	N,C,S	—	S, PSh, Sh	—	—

SWAMP SHRUBS

Scientific Name	Common Name	Range	Mature Height	Light Requirement	Wildlife Value	
					Food	Cover
Small Shrubs						
Hibiscus corcineus	Swamp hibiscus *	N,C,S	4-6 ft	S, PSh	M	M
Hypericum spp.	St. John's wort	N,C,S	3 ft	S, PSh	L	L
Itea virginica	Sweetspire	N,C	4-6 ft	S, PSh	L	L
Rhapidophyllum hystrix	Needle palm	N,C	6 ft	PSh	M	M
Large Shrubs						
Cephalanthus occidentalis	Common buttonbush *	N,C,S	20 ft	S, PSh, Sh	H	H
Clethra alnifolia	Summersweet clethra	N	10 ft	S, PSh	M	M
Cliftonia monophylla	Buckwheat tree	N	15-20 ft	PSh	M	H
Chrysobalanus icaco	Coco-plum *	S	15 ft	S	H	H
Cyrilla racemiflora	Titi or swamp cyrilla	N	10-25 ft	S, PSh	M	H
Forestiera acuminata	Swamp privet	S	50 ft	PSh, Sh	H	H
Fraxinus caroliniana	Carolina ash *	N	40 ft	PSh	H	H
Hamamelis virginiana	Witch-hazel	N	20-30 ft	S, PSh, Sh	L	H
Ilex coriacea	Giant gallberry	N	15 ft	S, PSh, Sh	H	M
Leucothoe racemosa	Hurrah-bush	N	24 ft.	S, PSh, Sh	?	?
Leucothoe racemosa	Staggerbush	C, S	30 ft.	S, PSh	?	?
Myrica cerifera	Southern wax myrtle	N,C,S	20 ft	S, PSh	H	H
Rhododendron serrulatum	Hammocksweet azalea	N	16 ft	S, PSh	M	M
Rhododendron viscosum	Swamp azalea	N	8-20 ft	S. PSh	M	M
Sabal minor	Dwarf palmetto	N,C,S	8 ft	S, PSh	M	M
Serenoa repens	Saw palmetto	N,C,S	10 ft	S, PSh	H	H
Viburnum nudum	Possumhaw	N,C,S	25 ft	S, PSh	H	H

RANGE:
   N = North Florida, C = Central Florida, S = South Florida
LIGHT REQUIREMENTS:
   S = Sun, Sh = Shade, PSh = Partial Shade
* = Plants characteristic of Coastal Strand
[T] = Toxic plant   [I] = Irritant plant

[S] = Example of plants that can be planted in shallow water (< 1 foot deep)
[D] = Example of plants that can be planted in deep water (1 to 4 feet deep)
WILDLIFE VALUES:
   L = Low, M = Medium, H = High

SWAMP TREES

Scientific Name	Common Name	Range	Mature Height	Light Requirement	Wildlife Value Food	Cover
Small Trees						
Alnus serrulata	Hazel alder	N,C	16 ft	S, PSh	L	H
Cornus foemina	Swamp dogwood	N,C,S	20 ft	PSh, Sh	H	M
Crataegus spp.	Hawthorne	N,C,S	15-20 ft	S, PSh	H	H
Ilex myrtifolia	Myrtle dahoon	N	25 ft	PSh	H	H
Nyssa ogeche	Ogeechee tupelo or lime	N	20-30 ft	S	H	H
Sambucus canadensis	Elderberry	N,C,S	20 ft	S, PSh	H	H
Viburnum obovatum	Walter viburnum	N,C,S	25 ft	S. PSh	H	H
Large Trees						
Acer negundo	Box elder	N,C	60 ft	S, PSh	H	H
Acer rubrum	Red maple *	N,C,S	40 ft	S	H	H
Annona glabra	Pond apple *	S	40 ft	S	H	H
Betula nigra	River birch *	N,C,S	75 ft	S	M	H
Carya aquatica	Water hickory *	N,C,S	60-100 ft	PSh	H	H
Celtis laevigata	Hackberry or sugarberry	N, C, S	50 ft	PSh	H	H
Chamaecyparis thyoides	Atlantic white cedar	N,C	30-90 ft	S	M	H
Diospyros virginiana	Common persimmon	N,C,S	30-60 ft	S	H	M
Gordonia lasianthus	Loblolly bay *	N, C, S	65 ft	S, PSh	M	H
Ilex cassine	Dahoon holly *	N,C,S	40 ft	S, PSh	H	H
Liquidambar styraciflua	Sweetgum	N,C,S	85 ft	S	L	H
Magnolia virginiana	Sweetbay	N,C,S	45 ft	S, PSh	H	H
Nyssa aquatica	Water tupelo *	N	30-50 ft	S	H	H
Nyssa sylvatica	Black gum	N,C,S	80 ft	S	H	H
Persea borbonia	Redbay	N,C,S	50 ft	S, PSh	H	H
Pinus serotina	Pond pine	N,C	40-70 ft	S	M	M
Planera aquatica	Water elm or planer tree	N	15-50 ft	S	H	L
Platanus occidentalis	American sycamore	N,C,S	100 ft	S	L	H
Quercus lyrata	Overcup oak	N	30-45 ft	S	H	H
Quercus nigra	Water oak	N,C,S	75 ft	S	H	H
Roystonea elata	Florida royal palm	C,S	100 ft	S, PSh	H	M
Sabal palmetto	Cabbage palm	N,C,S	60 ft	S, PSh	H	H
Salix caroliniana	Coastal plain willow	N,C,S	40 ft	S, PSh	L	H
Taxodium distichum	Bald cypress *	N,C,S	100 ft	S, PSh	L	M
Ulmus americana	American elm	N,C,S	60 ft	S	M	H

RANGE:
   N = North Florida, C = Central Florida, S = South Florida
LIGHT REQUIREMENTS:
   S = Sun, Sh = Shade, PSh = Partial Shade

* = Plants characteristic of Coastal Strand
WILDLIFE VALUES:
   L = Low, M = Medium, H = High

Freshwater Marsh Plant Tables

FRESHWATER MARSH GRASSES

Scientific Name	Common Name	Range	Mature Height	Light Requirement	Wildlife Value Food	Wildlife Value Cover
Amphicarpum myhlenbergianum	Little blue maidencane *	N,C,S	2 ft	S	—	—
Eragrostis elliottii	Elliott lovegrass	N,C,S	3 ft	S, PSh	—	—
Eustachys glauca	Saltmarsh chloris	N,C,S	3 ft	S	—	—
Leersia hexandra	Cutgrass *	N,C,S	3 ft	S	—	—
Muhlenbergia capillaris	Gulf muhly	C,S	2 ft	S, PSh	—	—
Panicum hemitomon	Maidencane *	N,C,S	6 ft	S, PSh	—	—
Phragmites australis	Common reed	N,C,S	6 ft	S, PSh	—	—
Spartina bakeri	Sand cordgrass	C,S	4 ft	S, PSh	—	—
Tripsacum dactyloides	Eastern gamagrass	C,S	6 ft	S, PSh	—	—
Zizaniopsis miliacea	Giant cutgrass	C,S	10 ft	S, PSh	—	—

FRESHWATER MARSH GRASSLIKES

Scientific Name	Common Name	Range	Mature Height	Light Requirement	Wildlife Value Food	Wildlife Value Cover
Carex spp.	Caric sedges	N,C,S	0.5-3 ft	S, PSh, Sh	—	—
Cladium jamaicense	Sawgrass	N,C,S	6 ft	S, PSh	—	—
Cyperus odoratus	Flatsedges	N,C,S	2 ft	S, PSh	—	—
Dichromena colorata	Star-rush	N,C,S	2 ft	S, PSh	—	—
Dichromena floridensis	White-top rush	N,C,S	2 ft	S, PSh	—	—
Eleocharis spp.	Spikerush S	N,C,S	0.5-2 ft	S, PSh, Sh	—	—
Fuirena scirpoidea	Umbrella grass	N,C,S	2 ft	S, PSh	—	—
Juncus spp.	Rush	N,C,S	3 ft	S, PSh	—	—
Phragmites australis	Common reed	N,C,S	6 ft	S, PSh	—	—
Rhynchospora spp.	Beakrush	N,C,S	2 ft	S, PSh	—	—
Scirpus americanus	Three square bulrush	N,C,S	3 ft	S, PSh	—	—
Scirpus californicus	Giant bulrush S	N,C,S	5 ft	S, PSh	—	—
Scirpus validus	Softstem bulrush S	N,C,S	4 ft	S, PSh	—	—

FRESHWATER MARSH HERBACEOUS

Scientific Name	Common Name	Range	Mature Height	Light Requirement	Wildlife Value Food	Wildlife Value Cover
Agalinis spp.	Gerardia	N,C,S	2 ft	S, PSh	—	—
Azolla caroliniana	Water fern	N,C,S	3 ft	S, PSh	—	—
Blechnum settulatum	Swamp fern	S	3 ft	S, PSh	—	—
Canna flaccida	Golden canna	N,C,S	2 ft	S, PSh	—	—
Conoclinium coelestinum	Mistflower	N,C	1-2 ft	PSh	—	—
Coreopsis spp.	Tickseed S	N,C,S	1-3 ft	S, PSh, Sh	—	—

(continued on next page)

RANGE:
   N = North Florida, C = Central Florida, S = South Florida
LIGHT REQUIREMENTS:
   S = Sun, Sh = Shade, PSh = Partial Shade
* = Plants characteristic of Coastal Strand

S = Example of plants that can be planted in shallow water (< 1 foot deep)
WILDLIFE VALUES:
   L = Low, M = Medium, H = High

(Freshwater Marsh Herbaceous continued)

Scientific Name	Common Name	Range	Mature Height	Light Requirement	Wildlife Value	
					Food	Cover
Crinum americanum	Swamp lily [S]	N,C,S	2 ft	S, PSh, Sh	—	—
Dichromena colorata	Star rush	N,C,S	2 ft	S, PSh	—	—
Eriocaulon spp.	Pipewort or hat pin	N,C,S	2 ft	S, PSh	—	—
Hymenocallis spp.	Spider lily	N,C,S	2 ft	S, PSh	—	—
Lachnanthes caroliniana	Red root	N,C,S	4 FT	S, PSh	—	—
Lachnocaulon spp.	Bog button	N,C,S	2 ft	S, PSh	—	—
Lobelia cardinalis	Cardinal flower [S]	N,C,S	2-6 ft	S, PSh	—	—
Nelumbo lutea	American lotus [D]	N,C,S	3 ft	S, PSh	—	—
Nuphar luteum	Spatterdock [D]	N,C,S	1 ft	S, PSh	—	—
Nymphaea mexicana	Yellow water-lily [D]	N,C,S	1 ft	S, PSh	—	—
Nymphaea odorata	Fragrant water-lily [D]	N,C,S	1 ft	S, PSh	—	—
Orontium aquaticum	Golden club [S]	N,C	0.5-1 ft	S, PSh	—	—
+Peltandra sagittifolia	White arum	N,C,S	2 ft	S, PSh	—	—
Peltandra virginica	Arrow arum [S]	N,C,S	2 ft	S	—	—
Pontedaria cordata	Pickerelweed * [S]	N,C,S	4 ft	S	—	—
Rhexia spp.	Knotweed	N,C,S	2 ft	S, PSh	—	—
Rudbeckia spp.	Coneflower	N,C,S	4 ft	S, PSh	—	—
Saggitaria spp.	Arrowhead [S]	N,C,S	2 ft	S, PSh	—	—
Saururus cernuus	Lizard's tail	N,C,S	2 ft	PSh, Sh	—	—
Sisurinchium spp.	Blue-eyed grass	N,C,S	1 ft	S, PSh	—	—
Thalia geniculata	Fire flag	C,S	2 ft	S	—	—
Vallisneria americana	Eelgrass	N,C,S	3 ft	S, PSh	—	—
Verbena spp.	Verbena	N,C,S	3 ft	S, PSh	—	—

FRESHWATER MARSH SHRUBS

Scientific Name	Common Name	Range	Mature Height	Light Requirement	Wildlife Value	
					Food	Cover
Cephalanthus occidentalis	Common buttonbush	N,C,S	20 ft	S, PSh, Sh	H	H
Myrica cerifera	Southern wax myrtle	N,C,S	20 ft	S, PSh, Sh	H	H

RANGE:
   N = North Florida, C = Central Florida, S = South Florida
LIGHT REQUIREMENTS:
   S = Sun, Sh = Shade, PSh = Partial Shade
* = Plants characteristic of Coastal Strand

[S] = Example of plants that can be planted in shallow water (< 1 foot deep)
[D] = Example of plants that can be planted in deep water (1 to 4 feet deep)
WILDLIFE VALUES:
   L = Low, M = Medium, H = High

Landscaping for Florida's Wildlife: Re-creating Native Ecosystems in Your Yard

Please help us evaluate and improve this book by answering the following questions.

1. I am a:

   _____ homeowner   _____ renter

   _____ other _____

2. Did you find this book well organized?

   _____ yes   _____ no

   If not, how could it be improved? _____

3. Is the reading level _____ too high?   _____ too low?   _____ just right?

4. Which feature(s) of the book did you find LEAST useful? Please explain.

5. Which feature(s) of the book did you find MOST useful? Please explain.

6. Does this book contain sufficient information?

   _____ yes   _____ no

7. This book would be more useful if

   _____ Additional content information were provided.

   _____ I had access to a demonstration area designed according to the information in this book.

8. How often do you use this book? _____

9. What is your overall evaluation of this book?

   _____ excellent   _____ very good   _____ good   _____ fair   _____ poor

10. Where did you obtain a copy of this book?

_____ gift

_____ book store, name _____

_____ University of Florida

_____ other _____

11. What other resources do you use to learn about wildlife and landscaping for wildlife?

Please mail the form to:

Dr. Joseph M. Schaefer
Wildlife Ecology and Conservation Department
University of Florida
PO Box 110430
Gainesville, FL 32611-0430

CHAPTER 5

Tools and Resources

If you'd like detailed descriptions of each major ecosystem, check them out.

***26 Ecological Communities of Florida* (revised 1989)**
Copies may be ordered from:
The Soil and Water Conservation Society
P.O. Box 2025, Gainesville, FL 32602
Phone: (352)338-9534 Fax: (352)338-9578
Contact: Bonita Rogers
($20 each, includes tax and shipping)

***Ecosystems of Florida* by Myers and Ewel**
University of Central Florida Press, 1990.
It is both more technical and more ecologically based than *26 Ecological Communities of Florida.*
It is $75 (hard cover) or $34.95 (paper) — both plus $3.50 shipping and applicable state sales tax
University Press
15 NW 15th Street, Gainesville, FL 32611
Phone: (800)226-3822 Fax: (352)392-7302

Wildlife and Ecosystem Resources — Local

Cooperative Extension Service
These federally, state and locally funded offices (one in each Florida county) are listed in the County or State government section of your phone book or on the Internet at
http://gnv.ifas.ufl.edu/WWW/AGATOR/HTM/CES.HTM

Wildlife and Ecosystem Resources — Regional

Northwest Florida Water Management District (NFWMD)
Rt. 1, Box 3100
Havana, FL 32333
(904)539-5999
URL: http://gcn.scri.fsu.edu/~bartond/

South Florida Water Management District (SFWMD)
P.O. Box 24680
West Palm Beach, FL 33416
(561)686-8800

Southwest Florida Water Management District (SWFMD)
2379 Broad Street
Brooksville, FL 34609
(352)796-7211

St. Johns River Water Management District (SJRWMD)
P.O. Box 1429
Palatka, FL 32177
(904)329-4500
URL: http://sjr.state.fl.us/

Suwannee River Water Management District (SRWMD)
Rt. 3, Box 64
Live Oak, FL 32060
(904)362-1001
email: srwmd@lo.gulfnet.com

Wildlife and Ecosystem Resources — Florida

Florida Department of Education
Office of Environmental Education
1311 Paul Russell Rd. Suite 201A
Tallahassee, FL 32301
(904)487-7900
FAX: (904)487-7908
URL: http://www.firn.edu/doe/doehome.htm

Florida Department of Environmental Protection
3900 Commonwealth Boulevard
Mailstop #30
Tallahassee, FL 32399-3000
(904)488-1554
URL: http://www.dep.state.fl.us/

Florida Division of Forestry
3125 Conner Boulevard
Tallahassee, FL 32399-1650
(904)488-4274
URL: http://thunder.met.fsu.edu/forestry/

Florida Game & Fresh Water Fish Commission
Schoolyard Program/Project WILD
620 South Meridian Street
Tallahassee, FL 32399-1600
(904)488-1960
URL: http://fcn.state.fl.us/gfc/gfchome.html

Environmental Information Center of the Florida
    Conservation Foundation
1251-B Miller Avenue
Winter Park, FL 32789
(407)644-5377

Florida Audubon Society
1331 Palmetto Ave. Suite 110
Winter Park, FL 32789
(407)539-5700
URL: http://www.audubon.org/audubon/florida.html
email: AudubonFla@aol.com

The Florida Native Plant Society
P.O. Box 6116
Spring Hill, FL 34606
(813)856-8202
URL: http://www.flmnh.ufl.edu/fnps/fnps.html

Florida Chapter of the Sierra Club
Wildlife Committee
103 Wildwood Lane
St. Petersburg, FL 33705
(813)821-9585
URL: http://www.sierraclub.org/
email: florida.chapter@sierraclub.org
        laurie.macdonald@sierraclub.org

Florida Wildlife Federation
P.O. Box 6870
Tallahassee, FL 32301
(904)656-7113

Florida Cooperative Extension Service: Wildlife
University of Florida
PO Box 110430
Gainesville, FL 32611-0430
(352) 846-0554
URL: http://www.wec.ufl.edu/extension

Wildlife and Ecosystem Resources — National

Ecological Society of America/Educational Section
Institute of Ecosystem Studies
P.O. Box R Attn.: Alan Berkowitz
Millbrook, NY 12545-0178
(914)677-5358 or (202)833-8773—general inquiries
URL: http://www.sdsc.edu/1/SDSC/Research/
  Comp_ Bio/ESA/ESA.html
email: esahq@esa.org

National Wildlife Federation
8925 Leesburg Pike
Vienna, VA 22184
(800)588-1650
URL: http://www.nwf.org/

Project WILD
National Office
5430 Grosvenor Lane
Bethesda, MD 20814
(301)493-5447
URL: http://eelink.umich.edu/wild/
email: natpwild@igc.apc.org

Wildlife Observations Recording Form

Copy the following recording form and use it to monitor changes (success) in the wildlife of your restored ecosystem.

Date	Time of day	Name	Wildlife Species			
			Count	Sex[a]	Age[b]	Comments[c]
12-12-97	4 PM	cardinal	2	M,F	Ad	feeding on ground

[a] M = Male, F = Female   [b] Ad = Adult, I = Immature
[c] you can include additional observations such as nest information, activity of animals (flying, perching, running, etc.), etc.

Template for Base Map

North

Scale

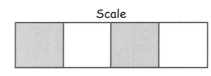

Plant and Non-plant Materials Cost Forms

Plant Materials Cost Form

Scientific Name	Common Name	Number	Size (gal)	Cost/ Plant	Total Cost
Grasses and herbaceous					
Vines					

Plant Materials Cost Form (continued)

Scientific Name	Common Name	Number	Size (gal)	Cost/ Plant	Total Cost
Small Shrubs					
Large Shrubs					

Plant Materials Cost Form (continued)

Scientific Name	Common Name	Number	Size (gal)	Cost/ Plant	Total Cost
Small Trees					
Large Trees					
Total Cost					

Non-plant Materials Cost Form

Name of Item	Number	Cost/Item	Total Cost
Burrows			
Bird Houses			
Bat Houses			
Treefrog Houses			
Bird/Squirrel Feeders			
Rock Piles			
Benches			
Signage			
Trail Materials (e.g. boardwalks, railings, weed barriers, mulch, etc.)			
Total Cost			

CHAPTER 6

Field Guides and Reference Books

The Golden Nature Guide Series

Publisher: Golden Press, c/o Western Publishing Company, Racine, WI 53404. 414/631-5258
Authors: various
Titles: *Golden Guide to Mushrooms*
Golden Guide to Insect Pests
Golden Guide to Pond Life
Golden Guide to Spiders and their Kin
Golden Guide to Butterflies and Moths
Golden Guide to Birds
Golden Guide to Nonflowering Plants
Golden Guide to Flowers
Golden Guide to Insects
Golden Guide to Trees
Golden Guide to Reptiles
Golden Guide to Mammals
Golden Guide to Fishes
Golden Guide to Weeds
Golden Guide to Seashells of the World
Golden Guide to Fossils
Golden Guide to Seashores

The Golden Field Guide Series

Publisher: Golden Press, c/o Western Publishing Company, Racine, WI 53404. 414/631-5258
Authors: various
Titles: *Birds of North America*
Trees of North America
Seashells of North America
Amphibians of North America
Reptiles of North America

National Audubon Society Field Guide Series

Publisher: Chanticleer Press, Inc., 568 Broadway, New York, NY 10012.
Authors: various
Titles: *Birds (Eastern Region)*
Birds (Western Region)
Butterflies
Fish, Whales, and Dolphins
Fossils
Insects and Spiders
Mammals
Reptiles and Amphibians
Rocks and Minerals
Seashells
Trees (Eastern Region)
Trees (Western Region)
Wildflowers (Eastern Region)
Wildflowers (Western Region)

The Peterson Field Guide Series

Publisher: Houghton Mifflin Company, Boston, MA 02116.
Authors: various
Titles: *A Field Guide to Birds*
A Field Guide to Shells of the Atlantic and Gulf Coasts and the West Indies
A Field Guide to Butterflies
A Field Guide to Mammals
A Field Guide to Animal Tracks
A Field Guide to the Ferns and Their Related Families of Northeastern and Central North America
A Field Guide to Reptiles and Amphibians of the United States and Canada East of the 100th Meridian
A Field Guide to Bird Nests (Found East of the Mississippi River)
A Field Guide to the Atlantic Seashore
A Field Guide to the Beetles of North America

Bird Guide for Florida Species

Kale, H. W. II, and D. S. Maehr. 1990. *Florida's Birds.* Pineapple Press, Sarasota, FL 34230. 941/953-2797

Amphibian and Reptile Guides for Florida Species

Ashton, R.E., Jr., and P.S. Ashton. 1981. *Handbook of Reptiles and Amphibians of Florida. Part One: The Snakes. Part Two: Lizards, Turtles, and Crocodilians. Part Three: The Amphibians.* Windward Publishing Company, Miami, FL 33137. 305/576-6232.

Ecosystem Restoration Through Landscaping

Cerulean, S., C. Botha, and D. Legare. 1986. *Planting a Refuge for Wildlife.* Florida Game and Fresh Water Fish Commission, Bureau of Nongame Wildlife, Tallahassee, FL 32399.

Dennis, J. V. 1985. *The Wildlife Gardener.* Alfred A. Knopf, New York, NY 10022.

Xerxes Society. 1990. *Butterfly Gardening.* Sierra Club Books, San Francisco, CA 94104.

Plant Identification

Bell, C. R. and B. J. Taylor. 1982. *Florida Wild Flowers and Roadside Plants.* Laurel Hill Press, Chapel Hill, NC 27516.

Foote, L. E. and L. B Jones, Jr. 1989. *Native Shrubs and Woody Vines of the Southeast.* Timber Press, Portland, OR 97204.

Duncan, W. H. and M. B. Duncan. 1988. *Trees of the Southeastern United States.* The University of Georgia Press, Athens, GA 30605.

Ponds

Ortho Books. 1988. *Garden Pools & Fountains.* Ortho Books, San Francisco, CA.

Allison, J. 1991. *Water in the Garden.* Little Brown & Co., New York, NY 10020.

Butts, D., J. Hinton, C. Watson, K. Langeland, D. Hall, and M. Kane. 1991. *Aquascaping: Planting and Maintenance.* Cooperative Extension Service Circular 912, IFAS, University of Florida, Gainesville, FL 32611.

Other References

Cornell, J. B. 1979. *Sharing Nature with Children.* Ananda Publications, Nevada City, CA.

Horwitz, E. (ed.). 1977. *Ways of Wildlife.* Citation Press/Scholastic, New York, NY.

Martin, A. C., H. S. Zim, and A. L. Nelson. 1951. *American Wildlife & Plants: A Guide to Wildlife Food Habits.* Dover Publications, Inc., New York, NY 10022.

Huegel, C. N. 1995. *Florida Plants for Wildlife.* The Florida Native Plant Society, Orlando, FL.

CHAPTER 7

Amphibians, Birds, Mammals, and Reptiles Found in Florida

What can you expect?

As you have already guessed, restoring your natural Florida ecosystem will make your property more likely to host all sorts of Florida critters. Which ones will pick your property? That's a question no one can answer.

However, the following tables will give you an idea of what you might expect: occasional or seasonal visitors—or more permanent guests—from 51 species of amphibians, 500 species of birds, 94 mammal species, and 88 species of reptiles!

Some of the factors affecting what shows up are local rainfall pattern (wet or dry season); air currents and/or weather patterns; seasons elsewhere (particularly true of migratory birds); critters' life cycle stage (mating, breeding, nesting, hatching, rearing, etc.); major natural and human dislocations such as hurricanes, tornadoes, major, long-standing construction projects, proximity to local natural areas, habitat values of your neighbors, etc.

Table 1. Of the *51 species of amphibians* that live in Florida, this table shows how some of the more common ones use different ecosystems for feeding and nesting/breeding.

Species	Ecosystems						
	CS[1]	SC[2]	SH[3]	HH[4]	FW[5]	SW[6]	FM[7]
Amphiuma Family							
Two-toed Amphiuma						fn	fn
Lungless Salamander Family							
Dwarf Salamander				f	f	fn	fn
Slimy Salamander				fn	f	fn	
Southern Dusky Salamander				f	f	fn	fn
Narrowmouth Toad Family							
E. Narrowmouth Toad	f	f	f	f	f	fn	n
Newt Family							
Peninsula Newt				f		fn	fn
Siren Family							
Eastern Lesser Siren						fn	fn
Greater Siren				fn	fn	fn	
Narrow-striped Dwarf Siren						fn	fn
Spadefoot Toad Family							
Eastern Spadefoot Toad	f	f	f	f	f	f	n
Toad Family							
Oak Toad	f	f	f		f	n	n
Southern Toad	f	f	f	f	f	fn	n
Treefrog Family							
Barking Treefrog	f	f	f			f	n
Florida Chorus Frog				f	f	fn	n
Florida Cricket Frog					fn	fn	
Green Treefrog				f	f	fn	fn
Little Grass Frog				f	f	fn	n
Pinewoods Treefrog	f	f	f	f	f	fn	n
Squirrel Treefrog	f	f	f	f	f	f	n
True Frogs							
Bullfrog						fn	fn
Florida Gopher Frog	f	f	f		f		n
Pig Frog						fn	fn
Southern Leopard Frog				f	f	fn	fn

[1] CS = Coastal Strand   [3] SH = Sandhill   [5] FW = Flatwoods   [7] FM = Freshwater Marsh   n = use ecosystem for nesting/breeding
[2] SC = Scrub   [4] HH = Hardwood Hammock   [6] SW = Swamp   f = use ecosystem to obtain food resources

Species	CS[1]	SC[2]	SH[3]	HH[4]	FW[5]	SW[6]	FM[7]
Ecosystems							
Barn-owl Family							
Common Barn Owl				fn	fn		
Bittern and Heron Family							
American Bittern							fn
Black-crowned Night Heron				n	n	fn	f
Cattle Egret	f	f	f	fn	fn	n	f
Eastern Least Bittern							fn
Great Blue Heron				n	n	fn	f
Great Egret				n	n	fn	f
Green-backed Heron						fn	f
Little Blue Heron				n	n	fn	f
Snowy Egret				n	n	fn	f
Tricolored Heron				n	n	fn	f
Yellow-crowned Night Heron				n	n	fn	f
Cormorant Family							
Double-crested Cormorant						fn	fn
Crane Family							
Sandhill Crane	f	f	f		f		n
Cuckoo Family							
Yellow-billed Cuckoo	fn	fn	fn	fn	fn	fn	
Darter Family							
Anhinga						fn	fn
Falcon Family							
Southeastern American Kestrel	fn	fn	fn		fn		
Flycatcher Family							
Eastern Kingbird	fn	fn	fn		fn		
Great Crested Flycatcher		fn	fn	fn	fn	fn	fn
Goose and Duck Family							
Mallard Duck							fn
Mottled Duck							fn
Wood Duck				n	n	fn	f
Grebe Family							
Pied-bill Grebe							fn
Hummingbird Family							
Ruby-throated Hummingbird				fn	fn	fn	
Ibis Family							
White Ibis				n	n	fn	f

(continued on next page)

---

[1] CS = Coastal Strand   [3] SH = Sandhill   [5] FW = Flatwoods   [7] FM = Freshwater Marsh   n = use ecosystem for nesting/breeding
[2] SC = Scrub   [4] HH = Hardwood Hammock   [6] SW = Swamp   f = use ecosystem to obtain food resources

Table 2 continued.

Species	Ecosystems						
	CS[1]	SC[2]	SH[3]	HH[4]	FW[5]	SW[6]	FM[7]
Jay and Crow Family							
American Crow	fn	fn	fn	fn	fn		
Blue Jay	fn	fn	fn	fn	fn	fn	
Fish Crow			fn	fn	fn	f	f
Florida Scrub Jay	fn	fn					
Kingfisher Family							
Belted Kingfisher	n	n	n	n	n	f	f
Kite, Eagle, and Hawk Family							
American Swallow-tailed Kite	fn	fn	fn	fn	fn	fn	f
Cooper's Hawk	fn	fn	fn	fn	fn		
Osprey		n	n	n	n	n	f
Red-shouldered Hawk				fn	fn	fn	
Red-tailed Hawk	fn	fn	fn	fn	fn		
Southern Bald Eagle	n	n	n	n	n	n	f
Limpkin Family							
Limpkin						fn	fn
Mimic Thrush Family							
Brown Thrasher				fn	fn		
Northern Mockingbird	fn	fn	fn	fn	fn		
Nightjar Family							
Chuck-will's-widow	fn	fn	fn	fn	fn		
Common Nighthawk	fn	fn	fn	fn	fn		
Old World Warbler and Kinglet Family							
Blue-gray Gnatcatcher				fn	fn	fn	
Eastern Bluebird			fn	fn	fn		
Pigeon and Dove Family							
Common Ground Dove	fn	fn	fn	fn	fn		
Mourning Dove	fn	fn	fn	fn	fn		
Plover Family							
Killdeer	fn	fn	fn		fn		f
Rail, Gallinule, and Coot Family							
American Coot							fn
Common Moorhen							fn
King Rail							fn
Purple Gallinule							fn
Shrike Family							
Loggerhead Shrike	fn	fn	fn		fn		
Stilt Family							
Black-necked Stilt							fn

(continued on next page)

---

[1] CS = Coastal Strand   [3] SH = Sandhill   [5] FW = Flatwoods   [7] FM = Freshwater Marsh   n = use ecosystem for
[2] SC = Scrub   [4] HH = Hardwood Hammock   [6] SW = Swamp   f = use ecosystem to obtain food resources   nesting/breeding

Table 2 continued.

Species	Ecosystems						
	CS[1]	SC[2]	SH[3]	HH[4]	FW[5]	SW[6]	FM[7]
Stork Family							
Wood Stork				n	n	fn	f
Swallow Family							
Northern Rough-winged Swallow	fn	fn	fn	fn	fn	fn	f
Purple Martin Swallow	fn	fn	fn	fn	fn	fn	f
Swift Family							
Chimney Swift	fn	fn	fn	fn	fn	fn	
Titmouse Family							
Carolina Chickadee	fn	fn	fn	fn	fn	fn	
Tufted Titmouse	fn	fn	fn	fn	fn	fn	
Turkey and Quail Family							
Northern Bobwhite	fn	fn	fn	fn	fn		
Wild Turkey	fn	fn	fn	fn	fn	f	
Typical Owl Family							
Barred Owl				fn	fn	fn	
Burrowing Owl	fn	fn	fn		fn		
Eastern Screech Owl	fn	fn	fn	fn	fn	fn	
Great Horned Owl	fn	fn	fn	fn	fn	fn	
Vireo Family							
Red-eyed Vireo				fn		fn	
White-eyed Vireo	fn	fn	fn	fn	fn	fn	
Yellow-throated Vireo				fn		fn	
Blackbird and Oriole Subfamily							
Boat-tailed Grackle					fn	fn	
Brown-headed Cowbird				fn	n	n	
Common Grackle				fn	fn		
Eastern Meadowlark					fn		
Orchard Oriole				fn	fn		
Red-winged Blackbird							fn
Cardinal Subfamily							
Northern Cardinal	fn	fn	fn	fn	fn	fn	
Blue Grosbeak				fn	fn		
Tanager Subfamily							
Summer Tanager				fn	fn		
Towhee and Sparrow Subfamily							
Bachman's Sparrow					fn		
Rufous-sided Towhee	fn	fn	fn	fn	fn		

(continued on next page)

---

[1] CS = Coastal Strand [3] SH = Sandhill [5] FW = Flatwoods [7] FM = Freshwater Marsh n = use ecosystem for
[2] SC = Scrub [4] HH = Hardwood Hammock [6] SW = Swamp f = use ecosystem to obtain food resources nesting/breeding

Table 2 continued.

Species	CS[1]	SC[2]	SH[3]	HH[4]	FW[5]	SW[6]	FM[7]
Ecosystems							
Wood Warbler Subfamily							
Common Yellowthroat				fn	fn	fn	fn
Northern Parula Warbler				fn		fn	
Pine Warbler	fn	fn	fn		fn		
Prothonotary Warbler						fn	
Yellow-throated Warbler				fn	fn		
Vulture Family							
Black Vulture	fn	fn	fn	fn	fn		
Turkey Vulture	fn	fn	fn	fn	fn		
Woodpecker Family							
Downy Woodpecker	fn	fn	fn	fn	fn	fn	
Hairy Woodpecker	fn	fn	fn	fn	fn	fn	
NorthernFlicker	fn	fn	fn	fn	fn	fn	
Pileated Woodpecker	f	f	f	fn	fn	fn	
Red-bellied Woodpecker	fn	fn	fn	fn	fn	fn	
Red-headed Woodpecker	fn	fn	fn	fn	fn		
Wren Family							
Carolina Wren				fn	fn	fn	

[1] CS = Coastal Strand [3] SH = Sandhill [5] FW = Flatwoods [7] FM = Freshwater Marsh n = use ecosystem for
[2] SC = Scrub [4] HH = Hardwood Hammock [6] SW = Swamp f = use ecosystem to obtain food resources nesting/breeding

Landscaping for Florida's Wildlife

Table 3. Of the *94 mammal species that live in Florida,* this table shows how some of the more common ones use different ecosystems for feeding and nesting/breeding.

Species	Ecosystems						
	CS[1]	SC[2]	SH[3]	HH[4]	FW[5]	SW[6]	FM[7]
Armadillo Family							
Nine-banded Armadillo	fn	fn	fn	fn	fn	f	
Cat Family							
Bobcat	fn	fn	fn	fn	fn	f	
Deer Family							
White-tailed Deer	fn	fn	fn	fn	fn	f	f
Fox and Coyote Family							
Gray Fox	fn	fn	fn	fn	fn	fn	
Red Fox	fn	fn	fn	fn	fn		
Free-tailed Bat Family							
Brazilian Free-tailed Bat	fn	fn	fn	fn	fn	fn	f
Mole Family							
Eastern Mole	fn	fn	fn	fn	fn		
New World Rat, Mouse, and Vole Family							
Cotton Mouse	fn	fn	fn	fn	fn		
Florida Mouse	fn	fn	fn		fn		
Hispid Cotton Rat	fn	fn	fn		fn		
Marsh Rice Rat							fn
Round-tailed Muskrat							fn
Opossum Family							
Opossum	fn	fn	fn	fn	fn	fn	fn
Pig Family							
Wild Boar	fn	fn	fn	fn	fn	f	f
Pocket Gopher Family							
Southeastern Pocket Gopher	fn	fn	fn				
Rabbit Family							
Eastern Cottontail Rabbit				fn	fn		
Marsh Rabbit							fn
Raccoon Family							
Raccoon	fn	fn	fn	fn	fn	fn	f
Shrew Family							
Least Shrew					fn		fn
Southeastern Shrew				fn		fn	
Squirrel Family							
Fox Squirrel	fn	fn	fn		fn		
Gray Squirrel	fn	fn	fn	fn	fn	fn	
Sherman's Fox Squirrel	fn	fn	fn		fn		
Southern Flying Squirrel	fn	fn	fn	fn	fn	fn	

(continued on next page)

---

[1] CS = Coastal Strand [3] SH = Sandhill [5] FW = Flatwoods [7] FM = Freshwater Marsh n = use ecosystem for nesting/breeding
[2] SC = Scrub [4] HH = Hardwood Hammock [6] SW = Swamp f = use ecosystem to obtain food resources

Table 3 continued.

Species	CS[1]	SC[2]	SH[3]	HH[4]	FW[5]	SW[6]	FM[7]
Twilight Bat Family							
Big Brown Bat				fn	fn	fn	f
Eastern Pipistrelle Bat				fn	fn	fn	f
Evening Bat	fn	fn	fn	fn	fn	fn	f
Rafinesque's Big-eared Bat	fn	fn	fn	fn	fn	fn	f
Red Bat				fn	fn		fn	f
Yellow Bat			fn	fn		fn	f
Weasel and Skunks Family							
Eastern Spotted Skunk	fn	fn	fn	fn	fn		
Long-tailed Weasel	fn	fn	fn	fn	fn	f	
River Otter						fn	fn
Striped Skunk	fn	fn	fn	fn	fn		

---

[1] CS = Coastal Strand   [3] SH = Sandhill   [5] FW = Flatwoods   [7] FM = Freshwater Marsh   n = use ecosystem for
[2] SC = Scrub   [4] HH = Hardwood Hammock   [6] SW = Swamp   f = use ecosystem to obtain food resources   nesting/breeding

Table 4. Of the *88 species of reptiles that live in Florida*, this table shows how some of the more common ones use different ecosystems for feeding and nesting/breeding.

Species			Ecosystems				
	CS[1]	SC[2]	SH[3]	HH[4]	FW[5]	SW[6]	FM[7]
Alligator Family							
American Alligator					n	fn	fn
Box and Water Turtle Family							
Florida Box Turtle	fn	fn	fn	fn	fn		f
Peninsula Cooter	n	n	n	n	n	f	f
Colubrid Family							
Brown Water Snake						fn	fn
Central Florida Crowned Snake	fn	fn	fn	fn	fn	f	
Corn Snake	fn	fn	fn	fn	fn		
Eastern Coachwhip	fn	fn	fn		fn		
Eastern Garter Snake					fn	fn	
Eastern Hognose Snake	fn	fn	fn	fn	fn		
Eastern Indigo Snake	fn	fn	fn	fn	fn	f	
Eastern Mud Snake				n	n	f	f
Florida Brown Snake				fn	fn	f	f
Florida Pine Snake	fn	fn	fn		fn		
Florida Scarlet Snake	fn	fn	fn		fn	f	
Florida Water Snake							fn
Green Water Snake						fn	fn
Kingsnake	fn	fn	fn	fn	fn	f	
North Florida Swamp Snake				n	n	f	f
Peninsula Ribbon Snake				n	n	f	f
Pine Woods Snake	fn	fn	fn		fn		
Rough Green Snake	fn	fn	fn	fn	fn	f	
Scarlet Kingsnake	fn	fn	fn	fn	fn		
South Florida Swamp Snake				n	n	f	f
Southern Black Racer	fn	fn	fn	fn	fn	f	
Southern Ringneck Snake				fn	fn	f	
Striped Crayfish Snake						fn	fn
Coral Snake Family							
Eastern Coral Snake	fn	fn	fn	fn	fn	f	
Iguanid Family							
Green Anole	fn	fn	fn	fn	fn	f	
Southern Fence Lizard	fn	fn	fn	fn			
Mud and Musk Turtle Family							
Florida Mud Turtle	n	n	n	n	n	f	f
Stinkpot	n	n	n	n	n	f	f
Striped Mud Turtle	n	n	n	n	n	f	f

(continued on next page)

---

[1] CS = Coastal Strand [3] SH = Sandhill [5] FW = Flatwoods [7] FM = Freshwater Marsh n = use ecosystem for nesting/breeding
[2] SC = Scrub [4] HH = Hardwood Hammock [6] SW = Swamp f = use ecosystem to obtain food resources

Table 4 continued.

Species	Ecosystems						
	CS[1]	SC[2]	SH[3]	HH[4]	FW[5]	SW[6]	FM[7]
Skink Family							
Broadhead Skink				fn		f	
Ground Skink	fn	fn	fn	fn	fn	f	
Peninsula Mole Skink	fn	fn	fn				
Southeastern Five-lined Skink	fn	fn	fn	fn	fn		
Softshell Turtle Family							
Florida Softshell	n	n	n	n	n	f	f
Tortoise Family							
Gopher Tortoise	fn	fn	fn		fn		
Viper Family							
Dusky Pigmy Rattlesnake					fn	f	f
Eastern Diamondback Rattlesnake	fn	fn	fn	fn	fn		
Florida Cottonmouth					n	n	f	f
Whiptail Family							
Six-lined Racerunner	fn	fn	fn	fn	fn		

[1] CS = Coastal Strand   [3] SH = Sandhill   [5] FW = Flatwoods   [7] FM = Freshwater Marsh   n = use ecosystem for
[2] SC = Scrub   [4] HH = Hardwood Hammock   [6] SW = Swamp   f = use ecosystem to obtain food resources   nesting/breeding